WHAT'S COOKING
Thai

Christine France

This is a Parragon Book
First Published in 2000

Parragon
Queen Street House
4 Queen Street
Bath BA1 1HE, UK

ISBN: 0-75254-045-9

Printed in Indonesia

ACKNOWLEDGEMENTS

Editorial Consultant: Felicity Jackson
Editor: Beverly LeBlanc
Photography: Colin Bowling, Paul Forrester and Stephen Brayne
Home Economist and Stylist: Vicki Smallwood

All props supplied by Barbara Stewart at Surfaces.

NOTE

Cup measurements in this book are for American cups.
All-purpose flour is measured in scooped cups. Tablespoons are
assumed to be 15ml. Unless otherwise stated, milk is assumed to be full fat,
eggs are medium and pepper is freshly ground black pepper.

Recipes using uncooked eggs should be
avoided by infants, the elderly, pregnant women and anyone
suffering from an illness.

Contents

Introduction

Anyone who has a love of Thai food will appreciate that it is a unique cuisine, distinctly different from the countries which border it geographically, but with many foreign influences. Many of its characteristics are due to climate and culture, but a history of many centuries of invasions and emigration has played a large part in shaping Thai cuisine.

The roots of the Thai nation can be traced back to the first century, in the time of the Chinese Han Dynasty, when the T'ai tribes occupied parts of South China, along valuable trade routes between the East and West. Over the years, the T'ai had a close but often stormy relationship with the Chinese, and eventually began to emigrate south to the lands of what is now northern Thailand, bordering Burma and Cambodia, then sparsely occupied by Buddhist and Hindu tribes.

Eventually, the T'ai established the independent Kingdom of Sukhothai (translated as 'dawn of happiness'), which eventually became known as Siam. The ports of Siam formed the entry to an important trade route, where ships from all over Europe and Japan docked in the coastal ports or sailed up the rivers bringing foreign foods, teas, spices, silks, copper and ceramics. It was the Portuguese who, in the sixteenth century, introduced the chilli to this part of the world, where the plants thrived and continue to thrive. Trade with Arab and Indian merchants was important, too, and many Muslims settled in Siam. The Kingdom of Siam survived until the twentieth century, when it became the constitutional Thai monarchy in 1939.

Present-day Thailand still reflects much of these centuries of mixed cultures, and the Thai people are independent, proud, creative and passionate. Their love of life is clear in the way they take pleasure in entertaining and eating. They love to eat, at any time of day, and the streets are lined with food vendors selling a huge variety of tasty snacks from their stalls, carts or bicycles all day long.

Thai people love parties and celebrations, and during their many festivals, the colourful, often elaborate and carefully prepared festive foods show a respect for custom and tradition. Visitors are entertained with endless trays of tasty snacks, platters of exotic fruits, and Thai beer or local whisky. When a meal is served, all the dishes are served up together, so the cook can enjoy the food along with the guests. Thais take pride in presenting food beautifully, often carving vegetables into elaborate shapes as garnishes. Their intricate and skilled artistry is an important part of Thai culture, and shows a deep appreciaton of beautiful things.

Everyday life in Thailand is closely tied to the seasons, marked by the harvesting of crops and vagaries of the monsoon climate. The Thai people take their food seriously, taking great care in choosing the freshest of ingredients and carefully balancing delicate flavours and textures. Throughout Thailand, rice is the most important staple food, the centre of every meal, and coconut, in its various forms, has an almost equal place. Cooks in every region are expert at making the very most of the food that's available locally, so the character of many classic Thai dishes will often vary, depending on the region.

FUNDAMENTALS OF THAI CUISINE

Essential ingredients when you're starting out to cook your own Thai cuisine are coconut, lime, chilli, rice, garlic, lemon grass, ginger root and coriander (cilantro), and with a basic supply of these you can create many typical Thai dishes. Although many recipes have long lists of ingredients, the methods are mostly simple enough for even an inexperienced cook to handle.

The main principle of Thai cooking is balance, the five extremes of flavour, bitter, sour, hot, salt and sweet, being carefully and skillfully balanced within a dish, or over several courses, each dish contributing part of the whole perfect balance of the entire meal.

TYPICAL THAI FLAVOURINGS:

BASIL

Three types of sweet basil are used in Thai cooking, but the sweet basil we can buy in the West also works well. Oriental food stores often sell the seeds for Thai basil, so you can grow your own.

CHILLIES

The many varieties of chilli vary in heat, from very mild to fiery hot, so choose carefully. The small red or green 'bird-eye' chillies often used in Thai dishes are very hot, so if you prefer a mild heat, remove the seeds. Red are generally slightly sweeter and milder than green. Larger chillies tend to be milder. Dried crushed chillies are used for seasoning.

COCONUT MILK

This is made from grated and pressed fresh coconut. It can be bought in cans and longlife packs, in powdered form or in blocks (creamed coconut). Coconut cream is skimmed from the top, and is slightly thicker and richer.

CORIANDER (CILANTRO)

This is a fresh herb with a pungent, citrus-like flavour, widely used in savoury dishes. Try to buy it with a root attached.

GALANGAL

A relative of ginger with a milder, aromatic flavour. Available fresh or dried.

GARLIC

Garlic is used whole, crushed, sliced or chopped in savoury dishes and curry pastes. Pickled garlic is another useful item and makes an attractive garnish.

GINGER

Fresh ginger root is peeled and grated, chopped or sliced for a warm spicy flavour.

KAFFIR LIME LEAVES

The leaves have a distinctive lime scent, and can be bought fresh, dried or frozen.

LEMON GRASS

An aromatic tropical grass with a lemony scent similar to lemon balm. Strip off the fibrous outer leaves and slice or finely chop the rest, or bruise and use whole. It can also be bought in dried powdered form.

PALM SUGAR

This is a rich, brown unrefined sugar made from the coconut palm, sold in solid blocks, and the best way to use it is to crush it with a mallet or rolling pin. Muscovado sugar is a good substitute.

RICE VINEGAR

Also called 'mirin', this sweet rice vinegar is used as a savoury flavouring. Sherry or white wine vinegar can be used as a substitute.

SOY SAUCE

Both dark and light soy sauces are used for seasoning, but light is saltier than dark. Light soy sauce is used mainly in stir-fries or with light meats. Dark soy sauce adds a mature rich flavour and colour to braised and red meat dishes.

TAMARIND PASTE

The pulp of the tamarind fruit is usually sold in blocks. This gives a sour/sweet flavour. Soak the pulp in hot water for 30 minutes, press out the juice and discard the pulp and seeds.

THAI FISH SAUCE

Called *nam pla*, this is used like salt for seasoning, and has a distinctive, intense aroma. It is made from salted fermented fish.

Snacks, & Starters Soups

The structure of a Thai meal is more flexible than in the West, with no starters (appetizers) and main courses as such; instead, soups, side dishes, noodles, rice and main dishes appear simultaneously. Small snacks or appetizers may be served as afternoon treats or offered to guests before they sit down for a meal.

Many of the recipes in this section are savoury snacks which are eaten at all times of day and at parties and celebrations. The Thais eat whenever they are hungry, and street vendors cater for this need with a huge and tempting array of wares from their stalls and bicycles – each street vendor has his own speciality of fast food, from crab cakes to spare ribs, steamed mussels or rice soup.

Soups are part of almost every Thai meal, including breakfast. Lunch is frequently a bowl of soup, often a thin stock-based broth, usually spiked with red or green chillies, and with the addition of fine noodles, rice, egg strips or tiny fish balls, meat balls or cubes of tofu. In restaurants, soups are often served in a large 'firepot' with a central funnel of burning coals to keep the contents hot.

Tiger Prawn Rolls with Sweet Soy Sauce

These crisp, golden-fried little mouthfuls are packed with flavour and served with a hot-and-sweet soy dip – perfect to stimulate appetites at the start of a meal, or as a tasty hot snack.

Serves 4

INGREDIENTS

DIP:
1 small red bird-eye chilli, deseeded
1 tsp clear honey
4 tbsp soy sauce

ROLLS:
2 tbsp fresh coriander (cilantro) leaves
1 garlic clove
1½ tsp Thai red curry paste
16 wonton wrappers

1 egg white, lightly beaten
16 raw peeled tiger prawns (jumbo shrimp) with tails
sunflower oil for deep frying

1 To make the dip, finely chop the chilli, then mix with the honey and soy and stir well; set aside for later.

2 To make the prawn (shrimp) rolls, finely chop the coriander (cilantro) and garlic, and mix with the curry paste.

3 Brush each wonton wrapper with egg white and place a small dab of the coriander (cilantro) mixture in the centre. Place a prawn (shrimp) on top.

4 Fold the wonton wrapper over, enclosing the prawn (shrimp) and leaving the tail exposed. Repeat with the other prawns (shrimp).

5 Heat the oil to 180°C/350°F, or until a cube of bread turns golden in 30 seconds. Fry the prawns (shrimp) in small batches for 1–2 minutes each until golden brown and crisp. Drain on paper towels and serve with the dip.

VARIATIONS

If you prefer, replace the wonton wrappers with filo pastry – use a long strip of pastry, place the paste and a prawn (shrimp) on one end, then brush with egg white and wrap the pastry around the prawns (shrimp) to enclose and fry.

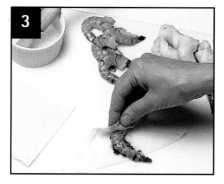

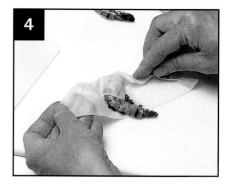

Prawn & Chicken Sesame Toasts

*A popular delicacy found throughout many countries in the East, these crisp,
golden fried toasts are very simple to make and perfect to serve with drinks at parties.*

Makes 72 pieces

INGREDIENTS

4 boneless, skinless chicken thighs
100 g/3½ oz cooked peeled prawns
  (shrimp)
1 small egg, beaten
3 spring onions (scallions), finely
  chopped

2 garlic cloves, crushed
2 tbsp fresh coriander (cilantro),
  chopped
1 tbsp Thai fish sauce
½ tsp ground black pepper
¼ tsp salt

12 slices white bread, crusts removed
75 g/2¾ oz/8 tbsp sesame seeds
sunflower oil for shallow frying
spring onion (scallion) curls, shredded,
  to garnish

1 Place the chicken and prawns (shrimp) in a food processor and process until very finely chopped. Add the egg, spring onions (scallions), garlic, coriander (cilantro), fish sauce, pepper and salt, and pulse for a few seconds to mix well; transfer to a bowl.

2 Spread the mixture evenly over the slices of bread, right to the edges. Scatter the sesame seeds over a plate and press the spread side of each slice of bread into them to coat evenly.

3 Using a sharp knife, cut the bread into small rectangles, making 6 per slice.

4 Heat a 1 cm/½ inch depth of oil in a wide frying pan (skillet) until very hot. Fry the bread rectangles quickly in batches for 2–3 minutes until golden brown, turning them over once.

5 Drain the toasts well on paper towels and serve hot, garnished with thinly shredded spring onion (scallion) curls.

COOK'S TIP

If you're catering for a party, it's a good idea to make the toasts in advance, then store them in the refrigerator or freezer. Cover and refrigerate for up to 3 days, or place in a sealed container or polythene (plastic) bag and freeze for up to 1 month. Thaw overnight in the refrigerator, then pop into a hot oven for about 5 minutes to reheat thoroughly.

Thai Fish Cakes with Hot Peanut Dip

These little fish cakes are very popular in Thailand as street food, and make a perfect snack. Or, serve them as a starter (appetizer), complete with the spicy peanut dip.

Serves 4–5

INGREDIENTS

350 g/12 oz white fish fillet without
   skin, such as cod or haddock
1 tbsp Thai fish sauce
2 tsp Thai red curry paste
1 tbsp lime juice
1 garlic clove, crushed
4 dried kaffir lime leaves, crumbled

1 egg white
3 tbsp fresh coriander (cilantro),
   chopped
salt and pepper
vegetable oil for shallow frying
green salad leaves, to serve

PEANUT DIP:
1 small red chilli
1 tbsp light soy sauce
1 tbsp lime juice
1 tbsp soft light brown sugar
3 tbsp chunky peanut butter
4 tbsp coconut milk

1 Put the fish fillet in a food processor with the fish sauce, curry paste, lime juice, garlic, lime leaves and egg white, and process until a smooth paste forms.

2 Stir in the coriander (coriander) and quickly process again until mixed. Divide the mixture into 8–10 pieces and roll into balls, then flatten to make round patties and set aside.

3 For the dip, halve and deseed the chilli, then chop finely. Place in a small pan with the remaining dip ingredients and heat gently, stirring constantly, until well blended. Adjust the seasoning to taste.

4 Shallow fry the fish cakes in batches for 3–4 minutes on each side until golden brown. Drain on paper towels and serve them hot on a bed of green salad leaves with the chilli-flavoured peanut dip.

Steamed Crab Cakes

These pretty little steamed and fried crab cakes are usually served as a snack, but you can serve them as a starter (appetizer) instead. In Thailand the banana leaves are skillfully shaped to make a container, but for ease of use you can use ramekins.

Serves 4

INGREDIENTS

1–2 banana leaves
2 garlic cloves, crushed
1 tsp lemon grass, finely chopped
½ tsp ground black pepper
2 tbsp fresh coriander (cilantro), chopped

3 tbsp creamed coconut
1 tbsp lime juice
200 g/7 oz/1½ cups cooked crab meat, flaked
1 tbsp Thai fish sauce
2 egg whites

1 egg yolk
8 fresh coriander (cilantro) leaves
sunflower oil for deep frying
chilli sauce dip, to serve

1 Use the banana leaves to line eight 100 ml/3½ fl oz/scant ½ cup ramekins or foil containers.

2 Mix together the garlic, lemon grass, pepper and coriander. Mash the creamed coconut with the lime juice until smooth. Stir it into the other ingredients with the crab meat and fish sauce.

3 In a clean, dry bowl, whisk the egg whites until stiff, then lightly and evenly fold them into the crab mixture.

4 Spoon the mixture into the ramekins or foil containers lined with banana leaves and press down lightly. Brush the tops with egg yolk and top each with a coriander (cilantro) leaf.

5 Place in a steamer half-filled with boiling water, then cover with a lid and steam for 15 minutes, or until firm to the touch. Pour off the excess liquid and remove from the ramekins or foil containers.

6 Heat the oil to 180°C/350°F, or until a cube of bread browns in 30 seconds. Add the crab cakes and deep fry for about 1 minute, turning them over once, until golden brown. Serve hot with a chilli sauce dip.

Thai-style
Open Crab Meat Sandwich

A hearty, open sandwich, topped with a classic flavour combination – crab with avocado and ginger. Perfect for a light summer lunch – or anytime!

Serves 2

INGREDIENTS

2 tbsp lime juice

2 cm/¾ inch piece fresh ginger root, grated

2 cm/¾ inch piece lemon grass, finely chopped

5 tbsp mayonnaise

2 large slices crusty bread

1 ripe avocado

150 g/5½ oz/1 cup cooked crab meat

black pepper, freshly ground

sprigs fresh coriander (cilantro), to garnish

1 Mix half the lime juice with the ginger and lemon grass. Add the mayonnaise and mix well.

2 Spread 1 tablespoon of mayonnaise smoothly over each slice of bread.

3 Halve the avocado and remove the stone (pit). Peel and slice the flesh thinly, then arrange the slices on the bread. Sprinkle with lime juice.

4 Spoon the crab meat over the avocado, then add any remaining lime juice. Spoon over the remaining mayonnaise, season with freshly ground black pepper, top with a coriander (cilantro) sprig and serve immediately.

COOK'S TIP

To make lime-and-ginger-flavoured mayonnaise, place 2 egg yolks, 1 tablespoon lime juice and ½ teaspoon grated ginger root in a blender goblet. With the motor running, gradually add 300 ml/ 10 fl oz/1¼ cups olive oil, drop by drop, until the mixture is thick and smooth. Season with salt and pepper.

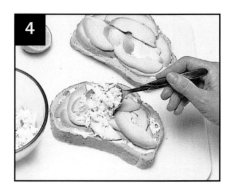

Mussels in Spiced Batter

*Little taste explosions – these make excellent nibbles to have with drinks before a meal,
as they really pep up appetites, and leave everyone wanting more.*

Serves 4

INGREDIENTS

40 large fresh mussels in shells
2 tbsp plain (all-purpose) flour
2 tbsp rice flour
½ tsp salt
1 tbsp desiccated (shredded) coconut

1 egg white
1 tbsp rice wine
2 tbsp water
1 small red bird-eye chilli, deseeded
  and chopped

1 tbsp fresh coriander (cilantro),
  chopped
sunflower oil for deep frying
lime wedges, to serve

1 Thoroughly clean the mussels and discard any that do not close when tapped or appear to be damaged. Rinse in cold water and place in a pan, cover and steam over a high heat for 2–3 minutes, shaking the pan occasionally, until the mussels open. Drain, then remove from the shells. Discard any that are not open.

2 For the batter, sift the plain (all-purpose) flour, rice flour and salt into a bowl. Add the coconut, egg white, rice wine and water, and beat the ingredients until well mixed and a batter forms. Stir the chilli and coriander (cilantro) into the batter.

3 Heat a 5 cm/2 in depth of oil in a large pan to 180°C/350°F, or until a cube of bread browns in 30 seconds. Holding the mussels with a fork, dip them quickly into the batter, then drop into the hot oil and fry for 1–2 minutes until crisp and golden brown.

4 Drain the mussels on paper towels and serve hot with lime wedges to squeeze over.

COOK'S TIP

If you reserve the mussel shells, the cooked mussels can be replaced in them to serve.

Steamed Mussels with Lemon Grass & Basil

Thai cooks are fond of basil, and frequently sprinkle it over salads and soups. The familiar sweet basil available in Europe and America is ideal for use in most Thai recipes, including this one.

Serves 4

INGREDIENTS

1 kg/2 lb 4 oz/5½ cups fresh mussels in shells
2 shallots, finely chopped
1 lemon grass stalk (stem), finely sliced

1 garlic clove, finely chopped
3 tbsp rice wine or sherry
2 tbsp lime juice
1 tbsp Thai fish sauce
25 g/1 oz/2 tbsp butter

4 tbsp fresh basil, chopped
salt and pepper
fresh basil leaves, to garnish
crusty bread, to serve

1 Clean the mussels, removing any beards and dirt. Rinse in clear water and drain. Discard any that do not close when tapped, or have damaged shells.

2 Place the shallots, lemon grass, garlic, rice wine, lime juice and fish sauce in a large pan and place over a high heat.

3 Add the mussels, cover with a lid and steam the mussels for about 2–3 minutes, shaking the pan occasionally during cooking until the mussel shells open.

4 Discard any mussels which have not opened, then stir in the chopped basil and season with salt and pepper.

5 Scoop out the mussels with a perforated spoon and divide between 4 deep bowls. Quickly whisk the butter into the pan juices, then pour the juices over the mussels.

6 Garnish each bowl with fresh basil leaves and serve with plenty of crusty bread to mop up the juices.

COOK'S TIP

If you prefer to serve this dish as a main course, this amount will be enough for two portions. Fresh clams in shells are also very good when cooked by this method.

Roasted Spare Ribs with Honey & Soy

Ideally, ask your butcher to chop the spare ribs into short lengths, about 6 cm/2½ inches long, so they're easy to eat with your fingers.

Serves 4

INGREDIENTS

1 kg/2 lb 4 oz Chinese-style spare ribs
½ lemon
½ small orange
2.5 cm/1 inch piece fresh ginger root, peeled
2 garlic cloves, peeled

1 small onion, chopped
2 tbsp soy sauce
2 tbsp rice wine
½ tsp Thai seven-spice powder
2 tbsp clear honey
1 tbsp sesame oil

lemon twists, to garnish
orange wedges, to serve

1 Place the ribs in a wide roasting tin (pan), cover loosely with foil and cook in an oven preheated to 180°C/350°F/Gas Mark 4 for 30 minutes.

2 Meanwhile, remove any pips (seeds) from the lemon and orange, and place them in a food processor with the ginger, garlic, onion, soy sauce, rice wine, seven-spice powder, honey and sesame oil. Process until smooth.

3 Pour off any fat from the spare ribs, then spoon the pureed mixture over the spare ribs.

4 Toss the ribs to coat evenly. Return the ribs to the oven at 200°C/400°F/Gas Mark 6 and roast for about 40 minutes, turning and basting them occasionally, or until golden brown. Garnish with lemon twists and serve hot with orange wedges.

COOK'S TIP

If you don't have a food processor, grate the rind and squeeze the juice from the citrus fruits, grate the ginger, crush the garlic and finely chop the onion. Mix these ingredients together with the remaining ingredients.

Steamed Wonton Bundles

These little steamed dumplings are served as a first course with a spicy dip. It's worth making a large batch and keeping a few in the freezer to thaw and cook as you need them.

Serves 4

INGREDIENTS

125 g/4½ oz minced (ground) pork
1 tbsp dried prawns (shrimp), finely chopped
1 green chilli, finely chopped

2 shallots, finely chopped
1 tsp cornflour (cornstarch)
1 small egg, beaten
2 tsp dark soy sauce

2 tsp rice wine
12 wonton wrappers
1 tsp sesame oil
salt and pepper

1 Mix together the pork, dried shrimp, chilli and shallots. Blend the cornflour (cornstarch) with half the egg and stir into the pork mixture with the soy sauce and rice wine. Season to taste with salt and pepper.

2 Arrange the wonton wrappers flat on a work surface and place about 1 tablespoon of the pork mixture on to the centre of each wrapper.

3 Brush the wrappers with the remaining egg and pull up the edges, pinching together lightly at the top and leaving a small gap so the filling can just be seen.

4 Put water in the bottom of a steamer and bring to the boil. Brush the inside of the top part with sesame oil.

5 Arrange the wontons in the top, cover and steam for 15–20 minutes. Serve hot, with a spicy dip.

COOK'S TIP

Make sure that the water in the base of the steamer is not allowed to go off the boil, or the dumplings will be undercooked and soggy. Also keep an eye on it so that it doesn't boil dry – top up with extra boiling water if necessary.

Crispy Pork & Peanut Baskets

These tasty little appetite-teasers are an adaptation of a traditional recipe that Thai cooks make with a light batter, but filo pastry is a good substitute that is much easier to handle.

Serves 4

INGREDIENTS

2 sheets filo pastry, each about
  42 x 28 cm/16½ x 11 inches
2 tbsp vegetable oil
1 garlic clove, crushed
125 g/4½ oz minced (ground) pork
1 tsp Thai red curry paste

2 spring onions (scallions), finely
  chopped
3 tbsp crunchy peanut butter
1 tbsp light soy sauce
1 tbsp fresh coriander (cilantro),
  chopped

salt and pepper
fresh coriander (cilantro) sprigs, to
  garnish

1 Cut each sheet of filo pastry into twenty-four 7 cm/2¾ inch squares, to make a total of 48 squares. Brush each square lightly with oil, and arrange the squares in stacks of 4 in 12 small patty tins (muffin pans), pointing outwards. Press the pastry down into the patty tins (muffin pans).

2 Bake the pastry cases in the oven preheated to 200°C/400°F/Gas Mark 6 for 6–8 minutes until golden brown.

3 Meanwhile, heat 1 tablespoon oil in a wok. Add the garlic and fry for 30 seconds, then stir in the pork and stir-fry over a high heat for 4–5 minutes until the meat is golden brown.

4 Add the curry paste and spring onions (scallions) and continue to stir-fry for a further 1 minute, then stir in the peanut butter, soy sauce and coriander (cilantro). Season to taste with salt and pepper.

5 Spoon the pork mixture into the filo baskets and serve hot, garnished with coriander (cilantro).

COOK'S TIP

When using filo pastry, remember that it dries out very quickly and becomes brittle and difficult to handle. Work quickly and keep any sheets of pastry you're not using covered with cling film (plastic wrap) and a dampened cloth.

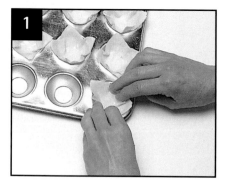

Sticky Ginger Chicken Wings

A finger-licking starter (appetizer) that's ideal for parties – but have some finger bowls ready. If you can't get chicken wings for this recipe, use drumsticks instead.

Serves 4

INGREDIENTS

2 garlic cloves, peeled
1 piece stem (candied) ginger in syrup
1 tsp coriander seeds

2 tbsp stem (candied) ginger syrup
2 tbsp dark soy sauce
1 tbsp lime juice

1 tsp sesame oil
12 chicken wings
lime wedges and fresh coriander
(cilantro) leaves, to garnish

1 Roughly chop the garlic and ginger. In a pestle and mortar, crush the garlic, stem (candied) ginger and coriander seeds to a paste, gradually working in the ginger syrup, soy sauce, lime juice and sesame oil.

2 Tuck the pointed tip of each chicken wing underneath the thicker end of the wing to make a neat triangular shape. Place in a large bowl.

3 Add the garlic and ginger paste to the bowl and toss the chicken wings in the mixture to coat evenly. Cover and leave in the refrigerator to marinate for several hours or overnight.

4 Arrange the chicken wings in one layer on a foil-lined grill (broiler) pan and grill (broil) under a medium-hot grill for 12–15 minutes, turning them occasionally, until golden brown and thoroughly cooked.

5 Alternatively, cook on a lightly oiled barbecue grill over medium-hot coals for 12–15 minutes. To serve, garnish with lime wedges and fresh coriander.

COOK'S TIP

To test if the chicken is cooked, pierce it deeply through the thickest part of the flesh. When fully cooked, the chicken juices are clear, with no trace of pink. If there is any trace of pink, cook for a few more minutes.

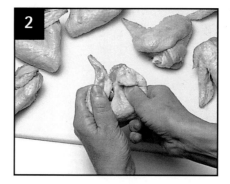

Stuffed Chicken Wings

The preparation of this dish is time-consuming, but worth the effort. With their unusual, typically Thai, savoury stuffing, the wings can be served hot or cold, and make a delicious picnic dish.

Serves 4

INGREDIENTS

8 chicken wings
3 tbsp dried prawns (shrimp)
3 tbsp hot water
200 g/7 oz minced (ground) pork
1 garlic clove, peeled and crushed
1 tbsp Thai fish sauce

½ tsp salt
½ tsp ground black pepper
2 spring onions (scallions), finely
  chopped
¼ tsp turmeric
1 small egg, beaten

2 tbsp rice flour
sunflower oil for deep frying
sweet chilli dipping sauce, to serve
fresh red chillies, to garnish
cucumber, sliced, to serve

1 Using a small sharp knife, cut around the end of the bone at the cut end of each wing, then loosen the flesh away from around the bone, scraping it downwards with the knife and pulling back the skin as you go. When you reach the next joint, grasp the end of the bone and twist sharply to break it at the joint. Remove the bone and turn back the flesh.

2 Continue to scrape the meat away down the length of the

next long bone, exposing the joint. Twist to break the bone at the joint and remove, leaving just the wing tip in place.

3 Meanwhile, soak the dried prawns (shrimp) in the hot water for 10–15 minutes. Drain, then chop. Place the pork, prawns (shrimp), garlic, fish sauce, salt and pepper into a food processor and process until it is a smooth paste. Transfer to a bowl and add the spring onions (scallions). Stir well.

4 Use the mixture to stuff the chicken wings, pressing it down inside with your finger.

5 Beat the turmeric into the egg. Dip each wing into the rice flour, shaking off the excess.

6 Heat a 5 cm/2 inch depth of oil in a large pan to 190°C/ 375°F, or until a cube of bread browns in 30 seconds. Dip the floured chicken wings quickly into the turmeric-flavoured egg, then drop carefully into the hot oil and fry in small batches for about 8–10 minutes, turning them over once.

7 Drain the chicken wings on paper towels. Garnish with fresh red chillies and serve hot or cold with sliced cucumber and a sweet chilli dipping sauce.

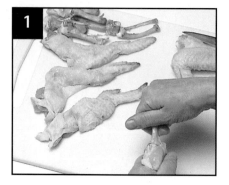

Lemon Grass Chicken Skewers

An unusual recipe in which fresh lemon grass stalks (stems) are used as skewers, which impart their delicate lemony flavour to the chicken mixture.

Serves 4

INGREDIENTS

2 long or 4 short lemon grass stalks (stems)
2 large boneless, skinless chicken breasts (halves), about 400 g/14 oz in total
1 small egg white

1 carrot, finely grated
1 small red chilli, deseeded and chopped
2 tbsp fresh garlic chives, chopped
2 tbsp fresh coriander (cilantro), chopped

1 tbsp sunflower oil
salt and pepper
coriander (cilantro) and lime slices, to garnish

1 If the lemon grass stalks (stems) are long, cut them in half across the middle to make 4 short lengths. Cut each stalk in half lengthways, so you have 8 sticks.

2 Roughly chop the chicken pieces and place them in a food processor with the egg white. Process to a smooth paste, then add the carrot, chilli, chives, coriander (cilantro) and salt and pepper. Process for a few seconds to mix well.

3 Chill the mixture in the refrigerator for about 15 minutes. Divide the mixture into 8 equal portions, and use your hands to shape the mixture around the lemon grass 'skewers'.

4 Brush the skewers with oil and grill (broil) under a preheated medium-hot grill (broiler) for 4–6 minutes, turning them occasionally, until golden brown and thoroughly cooked. Alternatively, barbecue over medium-hot coals.

5 Serve hot, and garnish with coriander (cilantro) and slices of lime.

COOK'S TIP

If you can't find whole lemon grass stalks (stems), use wooden or bamboo skewers instead, and add ½ teaspoon ground lemon grass to the mixture with the other flavourings.

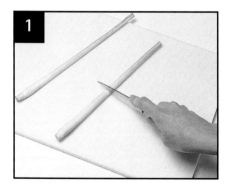

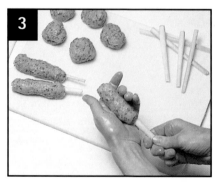

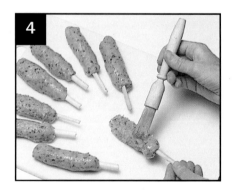

Chicken Roasted in Banana Leaves

Leaves such as banana are often used in Thai cooking as a natural wrapping for all kinds of ingredients. These tasty little appetizers will set everyone's taste buds jumping.

Serves 4–6

INGREDIENTS

1 garlic clove, chopped
1 tsp fresh ginger root, finely chopped
¼ tsp ground black pepper
2 sprigs fresh coriander (cilantro)

1 tbsp Thai fish sauce
1 tbsp whisky
3 boneless, skinless chicken breasts
 (halves)

2–3 banana leaves, cut into 7.5 cm/
 3 inch squares
sunflower oil for shallow frying
sweet chilli dipping sauces, to serve

1 Place the garlic, ginger, pepper, coriander (cilantro), fish sauce and whisky in a pestle and mortar and grind the ingredients to a smooth paste.

2 Cut the chicken into 2.5 cm/ 1 inch chunks and toss in the paste to coat evenly. Cover and chill in the refrigerator to marinate for about 1 hour.

3 Place a piece of chicken on a square of banana leaf and wrap it up like a parcel (package) to enclose the chicken completely.

Secure with wooden cocktail sticks (toothpicks) or tie with a piece of bamboo string.

4 Heat a 3 mm/⅛ inch depth of oil in a heavy-based frying pan (skillet) until hot.

5 Fry the parcels (packages) for 8–10 minutes, turning them over occasionally until golden brown and the chicken is thoroughly cooked. Serve with a sweet chilli dipping sauce.

COOK'S TIP

To make a sweet chilli dip to serve with the chicken pieces, mix together equal amounts of chilli sauce and tomato ketchup, then stir in a dash of rice wine to taste.

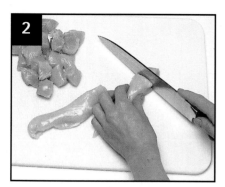

Chicken Balls with Dipping Sauce

*Serve these bite-sized chicken appetizers warm as a snack, with drinks
or packed cold for a picnic or lunchbox treat.*

Serves 4–6

INGREDIENTS

2 large boneless, skinless chicken
   breasts (halves)
3 tbsp vegetable oil
2 shallots, finely chopped
½ celery stick, finely chopped
1 garlic clove, crushed

2 tbsp light soy sauce
1 small egg
1 bunch spring onions (scallions)
salt and pepper
spring onion (scallion) tassels, to garnish

DIPPING SAUCE:
3 tbsp dark soy sauce
1 tbsp rice wine
1 tsp sesame seeds

1 Cut the chicken into 2 cm/¾ inch pieces. Heat half of the oil in a frying pan (skillet) or wok and stir-fry the chicken over a high heat for 2–3 minutes until golden. Remove from the pan with a perforated spoon; set aside.

2 Add the shallots, celery and garlic to the pan and stir-fry for 1–2 minutes until softened but not browned.

3 Place the chicken, shallots, celery and garlic in a food processor and process until finely minced (ground). Add 1 tablespoon of the light soy sauce, just enough egg to make a fairly firm mixture, and salt and pepper.

4 Trim the spring onions (scallions) and cut into 5 cm/2 inch lengths. Make the dipping sauce by mixing together the dark soy sauce, rice wine and sesame seeds; set aside.

5 Shape the chicken mixture into 16–18 walnut-sized balls.

Heat the remaining oil in the frying pan or wok and stir-fry the balls in small batches for 4–5 minutes until golden brown. As each batch is cooked drain on paper towels and keep hot.

6 Stir-fry the spring onions (scallions) for 1–2 minutes until they begin to soften, then stir in the remaining light soy sauce. Serve with the chicken balls and dipping sauce on a platter, garnished with the spring onion (scallion) tassels.

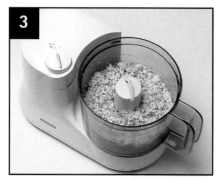

Stuffed Eggs
with Pork & Crab Meat

*These savoury stuffed eggs make a good picnic dish, or they can be popped into a lunchbox
for an unusual treat. Cool the eggs completely before packing.*

Serves 4

INGREDIENTS

4 large eggs
100 g/3½ oz minced (ground) pork
170 g/6 oz can white crab meat,
    drained
1 garlic clove, crushed
1 tsp Thai fish sauce

½ tsp lemon grass, ground
1 tbsp fresh coriander (cilantro),
    chopped
1 tbsp desiccated (shredded) coconut
100 g/3½ oz/⅔ cup plain (all-purpose)
    flour

about 150 ml/5 fl oz/⅔ cup coconut
    milk
salt and pepper
sunflower oil for deep frying
green salad, to serve
cucumber flower, to garnish

1 Place the eggs in a pan of simmering water and bring to the boil, then simmer for 10 minutes. Drain the eggs, crack the shells and cool under cold running water. Peel off the shells.

2 Cut the eggs lengthways down the middle and scoop out the yolks. Place the yolks in a bowl with the pork, crab meat, garlic, fish sauce, lemon grass, coriander (cilantro) and coconut. Season

with salt and pepper and mix the ingredients together thoroughly.

3 Divide the mixture into 8 equal portions, then fill each of the egg whites with the mixture, pressing together with your hands to form the shape of a whole egg.

4 Whisk together the flour and enough coconut milk to make a thick coating batter, seasoning with salt and pepper. Heat a 5 cm/

2 inch depth of oil in a large pan to 190°C/375°F, or until a cube of bread browns in 30 seconds. Dip each egg into the coconut batter, then shake off the excess.

5 Fry the eggs in 2 batches for about 5 minutes, turning occasionally, until golden brown. Remove with a perforated spoon and drain on paper towels. Serve warm or cold with a green salad garnished with cucumber flowers.

Thai-stuffed Omelette

This makes a substantial starter (appetizer), or a light lunch or supper dish.
Serve with a colourful, crisp salad to accompany the dish.

Serves 4

INGREDIENTS

2 garlic cloves, chopped
4 black peppercorns
4 sprigs fresh coriander (cilantro)
2 tbsp vegetable oil

200 g/7 oz minced (ground) pork
2 spring onions (scallions), chopped
1 large, firm tomato, chopped
6 large eggs

1 tbsp Thai fish sauce
¼ tsp turmeric
mixed salad leaves, tossed, to serve

1 Place the garlic, peppercorns and coriander (cilantro) in a pestle and mortar and crush until a smooth paste forms.

2 Heat 1 tablespoon of the oil in a wok over a medium heat. Add the paste and fry for 1–2 minutes until it just changes colour.

3 Stir in the pork and stir-fry until it is lightly browned. Add the spring onions (scallions) and tomato, and stir-fry for a further minute, then remove from the heat.

4 Heat the remaining oil in a small, heavy-based frying pan (skillet). Beat the eggs with the fish sauce and turmeric, then pour a quarter of the egg mixture into the pan. As the mixture begins to set, stir lightly to ensure that all the liquid egg is set.

5 Spoon a quarter of the pork mixture down the centre of the omelette, then fold the sides inwards towards the centre, enclosing the filling. Make 3 more omelettes with the remaining egg and fill with the remaining pork mixture.

6 Slide the omelettes on to a serving plate and serve with mixed salad leaves.

COOK'S TIP

If you prefer, spread half the pork mixture evenly over one omelette, then place a second omelette on top, without folding. Cut into slim wedges to serve.

Vegetarian Spring Rolls

These bite-sized vegetarian noodle-filled rolls are a tasty starter (appetizer)
to serve at the start of any meal with a sweet chilli dip.

Serves 4

INGREDIENTS

25 g/1 oz fine cellophane noodles
2 tbsp groundnut oil
2 garlic cloves, crushed
½ tsp fresh ginger root, grated
55 g/2 oz/⅔ cup oyster mushrooms,
   thinly sliced

2 spring onions (scallions), finely
   chopped
50g/1¾ oz/½ cup beansprouts
1 small carrot, finely shredded
½ tsp sesame oil
1 tbsp light soy sauce
1 tbsp rice wine or dry sherry
¼ tsp ground black pepper

1 tbsp fresh coriander (cilantro),
   chopped
1 tbsp fresh mint, chopped
24 spring- (egg-) roll wrappers
½ tsp cornflour (cornstarch)
groundnut oil for deep frying
fresh mint sprigs, to garnish

1 Place the noodles in a heatproof bowl, pour over enough boiling water to cover and leave to stand for 4 minutes. Drain, rinse in cold water, then drain again. Use scissors to snip into 5 cm/2 inch lengths.

2 Heat the groundnut oil in a wok or wide pan (skillet) over a high heat. Add the garlic, ginger, oyster mushrooms, spring onions (scallions), beansprouts and carrot and stir-fry for about 1 minute until just softened.

3 Stir in the sesame oil, soy sauce, rice wine, pepper, coriander (cilantro) and mint, then remove from the heat. Stir in the rice noodles.

4 Arrange the spring- (egg-) roll wrappers on a work surface, pointing diagonally. Mix the cornflour (cornstarch) with 1 tablespoon water and brush the edges of 1 wrapper. Spoon a little filling on to the pointed side of the same wrapper.

5 Roll the point of the wrapper over the filling, then fold the side points inwards over the filling. Continue to roll up the wrapper away from you, moistening the tip with more cornflour (cornstarch) mixture to secure the roll.

6 Heat the oil in a wok or deep frying pan to 180°C/350°F, or until a cube of bread browns in 30 seconds. Add rolls in batches and deep fry for 2–3 minutes each until golden brown and crisp. Serve hot.

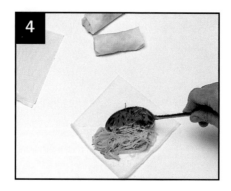

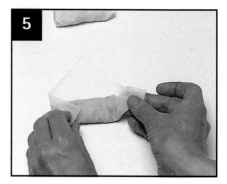

Sweet-and-Sour Seafood Salad

This unusual seafood dish with a sweet lime dressing can be a starter (appetizer) or doubled up for a buffet-style main dish, and is a good dish to prepare for a crowd if you're entertaining.

Serves 6 as a starter (appetizer)

INGREDIENTS

18 fresh mussels in shells
6 large scallops
200 g/7 oz baby squid, cleaned
2 shallots, finely chopped
6 raw tiger prawns (jumbo shrimp),
   peeled and deveined
¼ cucumber

1 carrot, peeled
¼ head Chinese leaves, shredded

DRESSING:
4 tbsp lime juice
2 garlic cloves, finely chopped
2 tbsp Thai fish sauce

1 tsp sesame oil
1 tbsp soft light brown sugar
2 tbsp fresh mint, chopped
¼ tsp ground black pepper
salt

1 Clean the mussels, discarding any damaged or open ones that do not close when firmly tapped. Steam them in just the water which clings to them for 1–2 minutes until opened. Lift out with a perforated spoon, reserving the liquid in the pan. Discard any mussels that have not opened.

2 Separate the corals from the scallops and cut the whites in half horizontally. Cut the tentacles from the squid and slice the body cavities into rings.

3 Add the shallots to the liquid in the pan and simmer over a high heat until the liquid is reduced to about 3 tablespoons. Add the scallops, squid and tiger prawns (jumbo shrimp) and stir for 2–3 minutes until cooked. Remove and spoon the mixture into a wide bowl.

4 Cut the cucumber and carrot in half lengthways, then slice thinly on a diagonal angle to make long, pointed slices. Toss with the Chinese leaves.

5 To make the dressing, place all the ingredients in a screw-top jar and shake well until evenly combined. Season with salt.

6 Toss the vegetables and seafood together. Spoon the dressing over the vegetables and seafood and serve immediately.

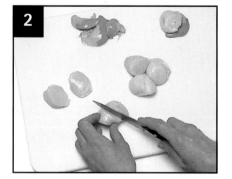

Warm Salad of Tuna & Tomatoes with Ginger Dressing

A colourful, refreshing first course that is perfect to make for a special summer lunch or dinner. The dressing can be made in advance and spooned over the dish just before serving.

Serves 4

INGREDIENTS

50 g/1¾ oz/½ cup Chinese leaves, shredded
3 tbsp rice wine
2 tbsp Thai fish sauce
1 tbsp fresh ginger root, finely shredded

1 garlic clove, finely chopped
½ small red bird-eye chilli, finely chopped
2 tsp soft light brown sugar
2 tbsp lime juice
400 g/14 oz fresh tuna steak

sunflower oil for brushing
125 g/4½ oz/1 cup cherry tomatoes
fresh mint leaves and mint sprigs, roughly chopped, to garnish

1 Place a small pile of shredded Chinese leaves on a serving plate. Place the rice wine, fish sauce, ginger, garlic, chilli, brown sugar and 1 tablespoon lime juice in a screw-top jar and shake well to combine evenly.

2 Cut the tuna into strips of an even thickness. Sprinkle with the remaining lime juice.

3 Brush a wide frying pan (skillet) or griddle with the oil and heat until very hot. Arrange the tuna strips in the pan and cook until just firm and light golden, turning them over once. Remove and set aside.

4 Add the tomatoes to the pan and cook over a high heat until lightly browned. Spoon the tuna and tomatoes over the Chinese leaves and spoon over the dressing. Garnish with fresh mint and serve warm.

COOK'S TIP

You can make a quick version of this dish using canned tuna. Just drain and flake the tuna, omit steps 2 and 3 and continue as in the recipe.

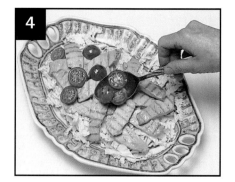

Chilli-spiced Prawn Wonton Soup

This delicious soup has a real kick of red-hot chillies, perfect to warm up a winter's day.
If you prefer a milder flavour, remove the seeds from the chillies before using them.

Serves 4

INGREDIENTS

WONTONS:
175 g/6 oz/1 cup cooked prawns
  (shrimp), peeled
1 garlic clove, crushed
1 spring onion (scallion), finely
  chopped
1 tbsp dark soy sauce
1 tbsp Thai fish sauce

1 tbsp fresh coriander (cilantro),
  chopped
1 small egg, separated
12 wonton wrappers

SOUP:
2 small red bird-eye chillies
2 spring onions (scallions)

1 litre/1¾ pints/4 cups clear beef
  stock
1 tbsp Thai fish sauce
1 tbsp dark soy sauce
1 tbsp rice wine
handful of coriander (cilantro) leaves,
  to garnish

1 Finely chop the prawns (shrimp). Put them in a bowl and stir in the garlic, spring onion (scallion), soy sauce, fish sauce, coriander (cilantro) and egg yolk.

2 Lay the wonton wrappers on a work surface in a single layer and place about 1 tablespoon of the filling mixture in the middle of each. Brush the edges with egg white and fold each one into a triangle, pressing lightly to seal. Bring the 2 bottom corners of the triangle around to meet in the middle, securing with a little egg white to hold in place.

3 For the soup, slice the chillies at a steep diagonal angle to make long thin slices, removing the seeds if you prefer. Slice the spring onions (scallions) on the same angle.

4 Place the stock, fish sauce, soy sauce and rice wine in a large pan and bring to the boil. Add the chillies and spring onions (scallions). Drop the wontons into the pan and simmer for 4–5 minutes until thoroughly heated.

5 Serve the soup and wontons in small bowls. Garnish with fresh coriander (cilantro) leaves scattered over at the last moment.

Hot & Sour Soup

Hot-and-sour mixtures are popular throughout the East, especially in Thailand. This soup typically has either prawns (shrimp) or chicken added, but tofu can be used instead if you prefer a meatless version.

Serves 4

INGREDIENTS

350 g/12 oz/2 cups whole raw or cooked prawns (shrimp) in shells
1 tbsp vegetable oil
1 lemon grass stalk (stick), roughly chopped
2 kaffir lime leaves, shredded

1 green chilli, deseeded and chopped
1.2 litres/2 pints/5 cups chicken or fish stock
1 lime
1 tbsp Thai fish sauce

1 red bird-eye chilli, deseeded and thinly sliced
1 spring onion (scallion), thinly sliced
salt and pepper
1 tbsp coriander (cilantro), finely chopped, to garnish

1 Peel the prawns (shrimp) and reserve the shells. Devein the prawns (shrimp), cover and chill.

2 Heat the oil in a large pan and stir-fry the prawn shells for 3–4 minutes until they turn pink. Add the lemon grass, lime leaves, chilli and stock. Pare a thin strip of zest from the lime and grate the rest. Add the grated rind to the pan.

3 Bring to the boil, then lower the heat, cover and simmer for about 20 minutes.

4 Strain the liquid and pour it back into the pan. Squeeze the juice from the lime and add to the pan with the fish sauce and salt and pepper to taste.

5 Bring the pan to the boil. Lower the heat, add the prawns (shrimp) and simmer for 2–3 minutes.

6 Add the thinly sliced chilli and spring onion (scallion). Sprinkle with the chopped coriander (cilantro) and serve.

COOK'S TIP

To devein the prawns (shrimp), remove the shells. Cut a slit along the back of each prawn (shrimp) and remove the fine black vein that runs along the length of the back. Wipe with paper towels.

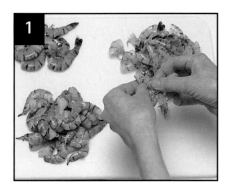

Creamy Sweetcorn Soup with Egg

This speedy soup is a good storecupboard (pantry) standby, made in a matter of minutes.
If you prefer, you can use frozen crab sticks, thawed and chopped,
or cooked prawns (shrimp) instead of canned crab meat.

Serves 4

INGREDIENTS

1 tbsp vegetable oil
3 garlic cloves, crushed
1 tsp fresh ginger root, grated
700 ml/1¼ pints/scant 3 cups chicken
  stock

375 g/13 oz can creamed sweetcorn
  (corn)
1 tbsp Thai fish sauce
170 g/6 oz can white crab meat,
  drained

1 egg
salt and pepper
fresh coriander (cilantro), shredded
  and paprika, to garnish

1 Heat the oil in a large saucepan and fry the garlic for 1 minute, stirring constantly.

2 Add the ginger to the pan, then stir in the stock and creamed sweetcorn (corn). Bring to the boil.

3 Stir in the fish sauce, crab meat and salt and pepper, then return the soup to the boil.

4 Beat the egg, then stir lightly into the soup so it sets into long strands. Simmer gently for about 30 seconds until just set.

5 Ladle the soup into bowls and serve hot, garnished with shredded coriander (cilantro) and pepper sprinkled over.

COOK'S TIP

To give the soup an extra rich flavour kick for a special occasion, stir in 1 tablespoon of dry sherry or rice wine just before you ladle it into bowls.

Pumpkin & Coconut Soup

This substantial soup is filling, and if served with crusty bread, is all you need for a satisfying lunch.
For a first course, serve in small bowls with a spoonful of spicy relish stirred into each portion.

Serves 6

INGREDIENTS

1 kg/2 lb 4 oz pumpkin
1 tbsp groundnut oil
1 tsp yellow mustard seeds
1 garlic clove, crushed

1 large onion, chopped
1 celery stick, chopped
1 small red chilli, chopped
850 ml/1½ pints/3¾ cups stock

1 tbsp dried shrimp, (prawns)
5 tbsp coconut cream
salt and pepper
extra coconut cream, to garnish

1 Halve the pumpkin and remove the seeds. Cut away the skin and dice the flesh.

2 Heat the oil in a large flameproof casserole and fry the mustard seeds until they begin to pop. Stir in the garlic, onion, celery and chilli, and stir-fry for 1–2 minutes.

3 Add the pumpkin with the stock and dried prawns (shrimp) and bring to the boil. Lower the heat, cover and simmer gently for about 30 minutes until the ingredients are very tender.

4 Transfer the mixture to a food processor or blender, and process until smooth. Return the mixture to the pan and stir in the coconut cream.

5 Adjust the seasoning to taste with salt and pepper and serve hot, with coconut cream swirled in each bowl.

COOK'S TIP

For an extra touch of garnish, swirl a spoonful of thick coconut milk into each bowl of soup as you serve it.

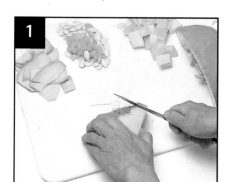

Mushroom & Tofu Broth

Dried black mushrooms are sold in Oriental stores, and although they can be expensive, they are worth searching out as they have a very specific aroma and flavour.

Serves 4

INGREDIENTS

4 dried black mushrooms
1 tbsp sunflower oil
1 tsp sesame oil
1 garlic clove, crushed
1 green chilli, deseeded and finely chopped

6 spring onions (scallions)
1 litre/1¾ pints/4 cups rich brown stock
80 g/3 oz/1½ cups fresh oyster mushrooms, sliced
2 kaffir lime leaves, finely shredded

2 tbsp lime juice
1 tbsp rice vinegar
1 tbsp Thai fish sauce
80 g/3 oz/½ cup firm tofu, diced
salt and pepper

1 Pour 150 ml/5 fl oz/⅔ cup boiling water over the dried black mushrooms in a heatproof bowl and leave to soak for about 30 minutes. Drain, reserving the liquid, then chop the black mushrooms roughly.

2 Heat the sunflower and sesame oils in a large pan or wok over a high heat. Add the garlic, chilli and spring onions (scallions) and stir for 1 minute until softened but not browned.

3 Add all of the mushrooms, kaffir lime leaves, stock and reserved mushroom liquid. Bring to the boil.

4 Stir in the lime juice, rice vinegar and fish sauce, lower the heat and simmer gently for 3–4 minutes.

5 Add the diced tofu and adjust the seasoning to taste with salt and pepper. Heat gently until boiling, then serve immediately.

COOK'S TIP

Use a clear, richly coloured home-made beef stock, or alternatively a Japanese dashi, to make an attractive clear broth. Stock (bouillon) cubes generally make a cloudy stock. To make a vegetarian version of the broth, use a well-flavoured vegetable stock and replace the fish sauce with light soy sauce.

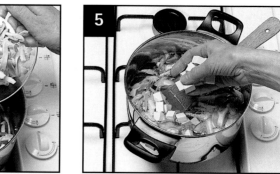

Rice Soup with Eggs

This version of a classic Thai soup, sometimes eaten for breakfast, is a good way of using up any leftover cooked rice, especially when you've cooked too much.

Serves 4

INGREDIENTS

1 tsp sunflower oil
1 garlic clove, crushed
50 g/1¾ oz minced (ground) pork
3 spring onions (scallions), sliced
1 tbsp fresh ginger root, grated

1 red bird-eye chilli, deseeded and
  chopped
1 litre/1¾ pints/4 cups chicken stock
200 g/7 oz/1¼ cups cooked long-
  grain rice

1 tbsp Thai fish sauce
4 small eggs
salt and pepper
2 tbsp fresh coriander, shredded, to
  garnish

1 Heat the oil in a large pan or wok. Add the garlic and pork and fry gently for about 1 minute until the meat is broken up but not browned.

2 Stir in the spring onions (scallions), ginger, chilli and stock, stirring until boiling. Add the rice, lower the heat and simmer for 2 minutes.

3 Add the fish sauce and adjust the seasoning with salt and pepper to taste. Carefully break the eggs into the soup and simmer over a very low heat for 3–4 minutes until set.

4 Ladle the soup into large bowls, allowing 1 egg per portion. Garnish with shredded coriander (cilantro) and serve.

COOK'S TIP

If you prefer, beat the eggs together and fry like an omelette until set, then cut into ribbon-like strips and added to the soup just before serving.

Spinach & Ginger Soup

This mildly spiced, rich green soup is delicately scented with ginger and lemon grass.
It makes a good light starter (appetizer) or summer lunch dish.

Serves 4

INGREDIENTS

2 tbsp sunflower oil
1 onion, chopped
2 garlic cloves, finely chopped
2.5 cm/1 inch piece ginger root, finely
    chopped

250 g/9 oz/4 cups fresh young
    spinach leaves
1 small lemon grass stalk (stem),
    finely chopped
1 litre/1¾ pints/4 cups chicken or
    vegetable stock

1 small potato, peeled and chopped
1 tbsp rice wine or dry sherry
1 tsp sesame oil
salt and pepper
 fresh spinach, finely shredded,
    to garnish

1 Heat the oil in a large saucepan. Add the onion, garlic and ginger, and fry gently for 3–4 minutes until softened but not browned.

2 Reserve 2–3 small spinach leaves. Add the remaining leaves and lemon grass to the saucepan, stirring until the spinach is wilted. Add the stock and potato to the pan and bring to the boil. Lower the heat, cover and simmer for about 10 minutes.

3 Tip the soup into a blender or food processor and process until completely smooth.

4 Return the soup to the pan and add the rice wine, then adjust the seasoning to taste with salt and pepper. Heat until just about to boil.

5 Finely shred the reserved spinach leaves and scatter some over the top. Drizzle with a few drops of sesame oil and serve hot, garnished with the finely shredded fresh spinach leaves.

VARIATION

To make a creamy-textured spinach and coconut soup, stir in about 4 tablespoons creamed coconut, or alternatively replace about 300 ml/10 fl oz/1¼ cups of the stock with coconut milk. Serve the soup with shavings of fresh coconut scattered over the surface.

Chilled Avocado, Lime & Coriander Soup

A delightfully simple soup with a blend of typical Thai flavours,
which needs no cooking and can be served at any time of day.

Serves 4

INGREDIENTS

2 ripe avocados
1 small mild onion, chopped
1 garlic clove, crushed
2 tbsp fresh coriander (cilantro), chopped
1 tbsp fresh mint, chopped

2 tbsp lime juice
700 ml/1¼ pints/scant 3 cups vegetable stock
1 tbsp rice vinegar
1 tbsp light soy sauce
salt and pepper

GARNISH:
2 tbsp soured cream or crème fraîche
1 tbsp fresh coriander(cilantro), finely chopped
2 tsp lime juice
lime rind, finely shredded

1 Halve, stone (pit) and scoop out the flesh from the avocados. Place in a blender or food processor with the onion, garlic, coriander (cilantro), mint, lime juice and about half the stock, and process until completely smooth.

2 Add the remaining stock, rice vinegar and soy sauce and blend again to mix well. Taste and adjust seasoning if necessary

with salt and pepper, or with a little extra lime juice if required. Cover and chill in the refrigerator until needed.

3 To make the lime and coriander (cilantro) cream garnish, mix together the soured cream, coriander (cilantro) and lime juice. Spoon into the soup just before serving and sprinkle with lime rind.

COOK'S TIP

The top surface of the soup may darken slightly if the soup is stored for longer than about an hour, but don't worry – just give it a quick stir before serving. If you plan to keep the soup for several hours, lay a piece of cling film (plastic wrap) over the surface to seal it from the air.

Meat Fish & Main Dishes

The Thais are primarily a fish-eating nation, and meat takes a back seat in most meals, except for special celebrations. The waterways of Thailand are teeming with many types of fish – even in the channels between the rice paddy fields – and the warm seas bring an abundance of fish and shellfish. So it's hardly surprising that along with rice, fish has long been a vital part of the Thai diet.

Even in the heart of Bangkok city, the markets are packed with fresh fish and seafood of all kinds. In Thai coastal towns, rows of thatch-roofed beach kiosks sell every type of fresh seafood from the warm Gulf waters, from barbecued or sautéed fish with ginger, prawns (shrimp) in coconut milk and coriander (cilanto), or steamed crab, to locals and visitors alike.

Because of the Thai Buddhist religion, which forbids the killing of animals, most butchers in Thailand are immigrant workers, such as the Chinese. Religion does not forbid eating meat, though it is often regarded as a special treat. Chicken is much more common than beef, and it's not unusual to see chicken, or sometimes pork, combined with seafood such as prawns (shrimp) or crab meat – a combination which works surprisingly well. Duck, another Thai favourite, is frequently barbecue-roasted with warm spices and soy or sweet glazes, much as in the Chinese style.

Stir-fried Beef with Beansprouts

A quick-and-easy stir-fry for any day of the week, this simple beef recipe is a good one-pan main dish. Serve a simple green side salad to complete the meal.

Serves 4

INGREDIENTS

1 bunch spring onions (scallions)
2 tbsp sunflower oil
1 garlic clove, crushed
1 tsp finely fresh ginger root, chopped
500 g/1 lb 2 oz tender beef, cut into thin strips
1 large red (bell) pepper, deseeded and sliced

1 small red chilli, deseeded and chopped
350 g/12 oz/3⅓ cups fresh beansprouts
1 small lemon grass stalk (stem), finely chopped
25 g/1 oz/2 tbsp smooth peanut butter

4 tbsp coconut milk
1 tbsp rice vinegar
1 tbsp soy sauce
1 tsp soft light brown sugar
250 g/9 oz medium egg noodles
salt and pepper

1 Trim and thinly slice the spring onions (scallions), setting aside some slices to use as a garnish.

2 Heat the oil in a frying pan (skillet) or wok over a high heat. Add the onions, garlic and ginger and then stir-fry for 2–3 minutes to soften. Add the beef and continue stir-frying for 4–5 minutes until browned evenly.

3 Add the (bell) pepper and stir-fry for a further 3–4 minutes. Add the chilli and beansprouts and stir-fry for 2 minutes. Mix together the lemon grass, peanut butter, coconut milk, vinegar, soy sauce and sugar, then stir this mixture into the wok.

4 Meanwhile, cook the egg noodles in boiling, lightly salted water for 4 minutes, or according to the packet (package) directions. Drain and stir into the frying pan (skillet) or wok, tossing to mix evenly.

5 Adjust seasoning with salt and pepper to taste. Sprinkle with the reserved spring onions (scallions) and serve hot.

Beef Satay with Peanut Sauce

Satay recipes vary throughout the East, but these little beef skewers are a classic version of the traditional dish. The deliciously more-ish peanut sauce turns the skewers into a rich, substantial dish.

Serves 4

INGREDIENTS

500 g/1 lb 2 oz beef fillet (tenderloin)
2 garlic cloves, crushed
2 cm/¾ inch piece fresh ginger root, finely grated
1 tbsp soft light brown sugar
1 tbsp dark soy sauce
1 tbsp lime juice
2 tsp sesame oil

1 tsp ground coriander
1 tsp turmeric
½ tsp chilli powder
chopped cucumber and red (bell) pepper, to serve

PEANUT SAUCE:
300 ml/10 fl oz/1¼ cups coconut milk
8 tbsp crunchy peanut butter
½ small onion, grated
2 tsp soft light brown sugar
½ tsp chilli powder
1 tbsp dark soy sauce

1 Cut the beef into 1 cm/½ inch cubes and place in a large bowl.

2 Add the garlic, ginger, sugar, soy sauce, lime juice, sesame oil, ground coriander, turmeric and chilli powder. Mix well to coat the pieces of meat evenly. Cover and leave to marinate in the refrigerator for at least 2 hours, or overnight.

3 To make the peanut sauce, place all the ingredients in a saucepan and stir over a medium heat until boiling. Remove from the heat and keep warm.

4 Thread the beef cubes on to bamboo skewers. Grill (broil) the skewers under a preheated grill (broiler) for 3–5 minutes, turning often, until golden. Alternatively, barbecue over hot coals. Serve with the sauce and chopped cucumber and red (bell) pepper pieces as garnish.

COOK'S TIP

The secret of success for this recipe is to cook the tender beef very quickly with a high heat, sealing in all the juices and flavour. Make sure the grill (broiler) or barbecue is very hot before you start to cook. Soak the skewers in cold water for about 20 minutes before threading the meat on to them – this reduces the risk of the skewers burning.

Beef & Peppers with Lemon Grass

A delicately flavoured stir-fry infused with lemon grass and ginger.
Colourful (bell) peppers help to complete the dish, and it's all cooked within minutes!

Serves 4

INGREDIENTS

500 g/1 lb 2 oz lean beef fillet
(tenderloin)
2 tbsp vegetable oil
1 garlic clove, finely chopped
1 lemon grass stalk (stem), finely
shredded

2.5 cm/1 inch piece fresh ginger root,
finely chopped
1 red (bell) pepper, deseeded and
thickly sliced
1 green (bell) pepper, deseeded and
thickly sliced

1 onion, thickly sliced
2 tbsp lime juice
boiled noodles or rice, to serve

1 Cut the beef into long, thin strips, cutting across the grain.

2 Heat the oil in a large frying pan (skillet) or wok over a high heat. Add the garlic and stir-fry for 1 minute.

3 Add the beef and stir-fry for a further 2–3 minutes until lightly coloured. Stir in the lemon grass and ginger and remove the wok from the heat.

4 Remove the beef from the pan or wok and keep to one side. Next add the (bell) peppers and onion to the pan or wok and stir-fry over a high heat for 2–3 minutes until the onions are just turning golden brown and slightly softened.

5 Return the beef to the pan, stir in the lime juice and season to taste with salt and pepper. Serve with noodles or rice.

COOK'S TIP

When preparing lemon grass, take care to remove the outer layers which can be tough and fibrous. Use only the centre, tender part, which has the finest flavour.

Red-hot Beef with Cashews

Hot and spicy, these quick-cooked beef strips are very tempting.
Serve them with lots of plain rice and cucumber slices to offset the heat.

Serves 4

INGREDIENTS

500 g/1 lb 2 oz boneless, lean beef
  sirloin, thinly sliced
1 tsp vegetable oil

MARINADE:
1 tbsp sesame seeds
1 garlic clove, chopped
1 tbsp fresh ginger root, finely chopped
1 red bird-eye chilli, chopped
2 tbsp dark soy sauce
1 tsp red curry paste

TO FINISH:
1 tsp sesame oil
4 tbsp unsalted cashew nuts
1 spring onion (scallion), thickly
  sliced diagonally
cucumber slices, to garnish

1 Cut the beef into 1 cm/½ inch wide strips. Place them in a large, non-metallic bowl.

2 To make the marinade, toast the sesame seeds in a heavy-based pan over a medium heat for 2–3 minutes until golden brown, shaking the pan occasionally.

3 Place the seeds in a pestle and mortar with the garlic, ginger and chilli, and grind to a smooth paste. Add the soy sauce and curry paste and mix well.

4 Spoon the paste over the beef strips and toss well to coat the meat evenly. Cover and leave to marinate in the refrigerator for 2–3 hours, or overnight.

5 Heat a heavy frying pan (skillet) or griddle until very hot and brush with vegetable oil. Place the beef strips over this and cook quickly, turning often, until lightly browned. Remove from the heat and spoon into a pile on a hot serving dish.

6 Heat the sesame oil in a small pan and quickly fry the cashew nuts until golden. Add the spring onions (scallions) and stir-fry for 30 seconds. Sprinkle the mixture on top of the beef strips and serve immediately garnished with cucumber slices.

Hot Beef & Coconut Curry

The heat of the chillies in this red-hot curry is balanced and softened by the coconut milk, producing a creamy-textured, rich and lavishly spiced dish.

Serves 4

INGREDIENTS

400 ml/14 fl oz/1¾ cups coconut milk
2 tbsp Thai red curry paste
2 garlic cloves, crushed
500 g/1lb 2 oz braising steak
2 kaffir lime leaves, shredded

3 tbsp kaffir lime juice
2 tbsp Thai fish sauce
1 large red chilli, deseeded and sliced
½ tsp turmeric
½ tsp salt

2 tbsp fresh basil leaves, chopped
2 tbsp fresh coriander (cilantro) leaves, chopped
shredded coconut, to garnish
boiled rice, to serve

1 Place the coconut milk in a large pan and bring to the boil. Lower the heat and simmer gently over a low heat for about 10 minutes until the milk has thickened. Stir in the red curry paste and garlic and simmer for a further 5 minutes.

2 Cut the beef into 2 cm/¾ inch chunks, add to the pan and bring to the boil, stirring. Lower the heat and add the lime leaves, lime juice, fish sauce, chilli, turmeric and salt.

3 Cover the pan and continue simmering for 20–25 minutes until the meat is tender, adding a little water if the sauce looks too dry.

4 Stir in the basil and coriander (cilantro) and adjust the seasoning with salt and pepper to taste. Sprinkle with coconut and serve with boiled rice.

COOK'S TIP

This recipe uses one of the larger, milder red chilli peppers – either fresno or Dutch – simply because they give more colour to the dish. If you prefer to use small Thai, or bird-eye, chillies, you'll still need only one as they are much hotter.

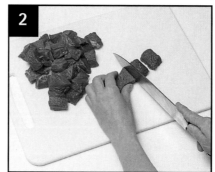

Roasted Red Pork

This red-glazed, sweet-and-tender pork, of Chinese origin, is a colourful addition to many stir-fries, salads and soups. Alternatively, simply serve it sliced and arranged on a wide platter over a bed of Chinese leaves.

Serves 4

INGREDIENTS

600 g/1 lb 5 oz pork fillets
   (tenderloins)
Chinese leaves, shredded to serve
red chilli flower, to garnish

MARINADE:
2 garlic cloves, crushed
1 tbsp fresh ginger root, grated
1 tbsp light soy sauce
1 tbsp Thai fish sauce
1 tbsp rice wine
1 tbsp hoi-sin sauce

1 tbsp sesame oil
1 tbsp palm sugar or soft brown
   sugar
½ tsp five-spice powder
a few drops red food colouring
   (optional)

1 Mix all the ingredients for the marinade together and spread over the pork, turning to coat evenly. Place in a large dish, cover and leave in the refrigerator to marinate overnight.

2 Place a rack in a roasting tin (pan), then half-fill the tin (pan) with boiling water. Lift the pork from the marinade and place on the rack. Reserve the marinade for later use.

3 Roast in a preheated oven at 220°C/425°F/Gas Mark 7 for about 20 minutes. Baste with the marinade, then lower the heat to 180°C/350°F/Gas Mark 4 and continue roasting for a further 35–40 minutes, basting occasionally with the marinade, until the pork is a rich reddish brown and thoroughly cooked.

4 Cut the pork into slices and serve on a bed of shredded Chinese leaves, garnished with a red chilli flower.

COOK'S TIP

The pork may also be grilled (broiled). Cut the meat into slices or strips and coat in the marinade, then arrange on a foil-lined grill (broiler) pan and grill (broil) under a high heat, turning occasionally and basting with marinade.

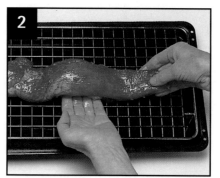

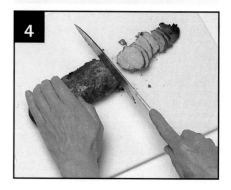

Pork with Soy & Sesame Glaze

Thai cooks are fond of adding sweet flavours to meat, as in this unusual pork dish, with soy and garlic to balance the sweetness of the honey. Pork fillet (tenderloin) is a very lean meat, so take care not to overcook or it will become dry.

Serves 4

INGREDIENTS

2 pork fillets (tenderloins), about 275 g/9½ oz each
2 tbsp dark soy sauce

2 tbsp clear honey
2 garlic cloves, crushed
1 tbsp sesame seeds
1 onion, thinly sliced in rings

1 tbsp seasoned plain (all-purpose) flour
sunflower oil, to fry
crisp salad, to serve

1 Trim the pork fillets (tenderloins) and place them in a wide non-metallic dish.

2 Mix together the soy sauce, honey and garlic. Spread this mixture over the pork, turning the meat to coat it evenly.

3 Lift the pork fillets (tenderloin) into a roasting tin (pan) or shallow ovenproof dish. Sprinkle evenly with sesame seeds.

4 Roast the pork in an oven preheated at 200°C/400°F/ Gas Mark 6 for about 20 minutes, spooning over any juices. Cover loosely with foil to prevent over-browning and roast for a further 10–15 minutes until the meat is thoroughly cooked.

5 Meanwhile, dip the onion slices in the flour and shake off the excess. Heat the oil and fry the onion rings until golden and crisp, turning occasionally. Serve the pork in slices with the fried onions on a bed of crisp salad.

COOK'S TIP

This pork is also excellent served cold, and it's a good choice for picnics, especially served with a spicy sambal (see page 162) or chilli relish.

Stir-fried Pork and Corn

A speedy dish, typical of Thai street food. This includes fresh sweetcorn, which, although introduced relatively recently to Thailand, is a very popular vegetable used in many dishes. Fresh sweetcorn (corn) from the cob, the fresher the better, is first choice, but if it's not available, use drained, canned sweetcorn instead.

Serves 4

INGREDIENTS

2 tbsp vegetable oil
500 g/1 lb 2 oz lean boneless pork, cut in thin strips
1 garlic clove, chopped
350 g/12 oz/2 cups fresh sweetcorn (corn) kernels

200 g/7 oz/1½ cups French (green) beans, cut into short lengths
2 spring onions (scallions), chopped
1 small red chilli, chopped
1 tsp sugar
1 tbsp light soy sauce

3 tbsp fresh coriander (cilantro), chopped
egg noodles or boiled rice, to serve

1 Heat the oil in a large frying pan (skillet) or wok and stir-fry the pork quickly over a high heat until lightly browned.

2 Stir in the garlic, sweetcorn, beans, spring onions (scallions) and chilli, and continue stir-frying over a high heat for 2–3 minutes, until the vegetables are heated through and almost tender.

3 Stir in the sugar and soy sauce stir-fry for a further 30 seconds, over a high heat.

4 Sprinkle with the coriander (cilantro) and serve immediately either with egg noodles or rice.

COOK'S TIP

In Thailand, long beans would be used for dishes such as this, but you can substitute French (green) beans, which are more easily available. But look out for long beans in Oriental food stores – they are like long string beans and have a similar flavour, but their texture is crisp, and they cook more quickly.

Spicy Fried Minced Pork

A warmly spiced dish, this is ideal for a quick family meal. Just cook fine egg noodles for an accompaniment while the meat sizzles, and dinner can be on the table in a matter of minutes!

Serves 4

INGREDIENTS

2 garlic cloves

3 shallots

2.5 cm/1 inch piece fresh ginger root, finely chopped

2 tbsp sunflower oil

500 g/1 lb 2 oz lean minced (ground) pork

2 tbsp Thai fish sauce

1 tbsp dark soy sauce

1 tbsp Thai red curry paste

4 dried kaffir lime leaves, crumbled

4 plum tomatoes, chopped

3 tbsp fresh coriander (cilantro), chopped

salt and pepper

boiled fine egg noodles, to serve

fresh coriander (cilantro) sprigs, to garnish

1 Peel and finely chop the garlic, shallots and ginger. Heat the oil in a wok over a medium heat. Add the garlic, shallots and ginger and stir-fry for about 2 minutes. Stir in the pork and continue stir-frying until golden brown.

2 Stir in the fish sauce, soy sauce, curry paste and lime leaves, and stir-fry for a further 1–2 minutes over a high heat.

3 Add the tomatoes and cook for a further 5–6 minutes, stirring occasionally.

4 Stir in the chopped coriander (cilantro) and season to taste with salt and pepper. Serve hot, spooned on to boiled fine egg noodles, garnished with coriander sprigs.

COOK'S TIP

Dried kaffir lime leaves are a useful storecupboard (pantry) ingredient as they can be crumbled easily straight into quick dishes such as this. If you prefer to use fresh kaffir lime leaves, shred them finely and add to the dish.

Thai-spiced Sausages

These mildly spiced little sausages are a good choice for a buffet meal.
They can be made a day in advance, and are equally good served hot or cold.

Serves 4

INGREDIENTS

400 g/14 oz lean minced (ground)
  pork
50 g/1¾ oz/4 tbsp cooked rice
1 garlic clove, crushed
1 tsp Thai red curry paste

1 tsp ground black pepper
1 tsp ground coriander
½ tsp salt
3 tbsp lime juice

2 tbsp fresh coriander (cilantro),
  chopped
3 tbsp groundnut oil
coconut sambal or soy sauce, to serve

1 Place the pork, rice, garlic, curry paste, pepper, ground coriander, salt, lime juice and chopped coriander (cilantro) in a bowl and knead together with your hands to mix evenly.

2 Use your hands to shape the mixture into 12 small sausage (link) shapes. If you can buy sausage casings, fill the casings and twist at intervals to separate the sausages.

3 Heat the oil in a large frying pan (skillet) over a medium heat. Add the sausages in batches if necessary, and fry for 8–10 minutes, turning them over occasionally, until they are evenly golden brown. Serve hot with a coconut sambal or soy sauce.

COOK'S TIP

These sausages can also be served as a starter (appetizer) – shape the mixture slightly smaller to make about 16 bite-sized sausages. Serve with a soy dip.

Thai-style Burgers

If your family likes to eat burgers, try these – they have a much more interesting flavour than conventional hamburgers!

Serves 4

INGREDIENTS

1 small lemon grass stalk (stem)
1 small red chilli, deseeded
2 garlic cloves, peeled
2 spring onions (scallions)
200 g/7 oz/2½ cups closed-cup
   mushrooms

400 g/14 oz minced (ground) pork
1 tbsp Thai fish sauce
3 tbsp fresh coriander (cilantro),
   chopped
sunflower oil for shallow frying
2 tbsp mayonnaise

1 tbsp lime juice
salt and pepper

TO SERVE:
4 sesame hamburger buns
shredded Chinese leaves

1 Place the lemon grass, chilli, garlic and spring onions (scallions) in a food processor and process to a smooth paste. Add the mushrooms and process until very finely chopped.

2 Add the minced (ground) pork, fish sauce and coriander (cilantro). Season well with salt and pepper, then divide the mixture into 4 equal portions and shape with lightly floured hands into flat burger shapes.

3 Heat the oil in a frying pan (skillet) over a medium heat. Add the burgers and fry for 6–8 minutes until done or as you like.

4 Meanwhile, mix the mayonnaise with the lime juice. Split the hamburger buns and spread the lime-flavoured mayonnaise on the cut surfaces. Add a few shredded Chinese leaves, top with a burger and sandwich together. Serve immediately, while still hot.

COOK'S TIP

You can add a spoonful of your favourite relish to each burger, or alternatively, add a few pieces of crisp pickled vegetables for a change of texture (see page 160).

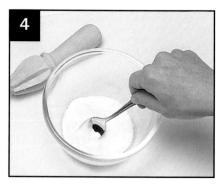

Red Lamb Curry

*This richly spiced curry uses the typically red-hot chilli flavour of Thai red curry paste,
made with dried red chillies, to give it a warm, russet-red colour.*

Serves 4

INGREDIENTS

500 g/1 lb 2 oz boneless lean
   leg of lamb
2 tbsp vegetable oil
1 large onion, sliced
2 garlic cloves, crushed
2 tbsp Thai red curry paste
150 ml/5 fl oz/⅔ cup coconut milk

1 tbsp soft light brown sugar
1 large red (bell) pepper, deseeded and
   thickly sliced
120 ml/4 fl oz/½ cup lamb or beef
   stock
1 tbsp Thai fish sauce
2 tbsp lime juice

227 g/8 oz can water chestnuts,
   drained
2 tbsp fresh coriander (cilantro),
   chopped
2 tbsp fresh basil, chopped
salt and pepper
boiled jasmine rice, to serve
fresh basil leaves, to garnish

1 Trim the meat and cut it into 3 cm/1¼ inch cubes. Heat the oil in a large frying pan (skillet) or wok over a high heat and stir-fry the onion and garlic for 2–3 minutes to soften. Add the meat and fry the mixture quickly until lightly browned.

2 Stir in the curry paste and cook for a few seconds, then add the coconut milk and sugar and bring to the boil. Reduce the heat and simmer for 15 minutes, stirring occasionally.

3 Stir in the red (bell) pepper, stock, fish sauce and lime juice, cover and continue simmering for a further 15 minutes, or until the meat is tender.

4 Add the water chestnuts, coriander (cilantro) and basil, adjust the seasoning to taste. Serve with jasmine rice garnished with fresh basil leaves.

COOK'S TIP

This curry can also be made with other lean red meats. Try replacing the lamb with trimmed duck breasts or pieces of lean braising beef.

Roast Chicken with Ginger & Lime

This is a version of a sweet-and-sour chicken dish often sold by street traders in the East –
they barbecue the chickens whole or cut in half, then chop them into pieces to sell.
Begin the preparation the day before you cook, or at least early in the day,
to give the flavours plenty of time to penetrate the chicken.

Serves 4

INGREDIENTS

3 cm/1¼ inch piece fresh ginger root,
  finely chopped
2 garlic cloves, finely chopped
1 small onion, finely chopped
1 lemon grass stalk (stem), finely
  chopped

½ tsp salt
1 tsp black peppercorns
1.5 kg/3 lb 5 oz roasting chicken
1 tbsp coconut cream
2 tbsp lime juice
2 tbsp clear honey

1 tsp cornflour (cornstarch)
2 tsp water
stir-fried vegetables, to serve

1 Put the ginger, garlic, onion, lemon grass, salt and peppercorns in a pestle and mortar and crush to form a smooth paste.

2 Cut the chicken in half lengthways, using poultry shears or strong kitchen scissors. Spread the paste all over the chicken, both inside and out, and spread it on to the flesh under the breast skin. Cover and chill overnight, or at least several hours.

3 In a small pan, heat the coconut cream, lime juice and honey together, stirring until smooth. Brush a little of the mixture evenly over the chicken.

4 Place the chicken halves on a tray over a roasting tin (pan) half-filled with boiling water. Roast in an oven preheated to 180°C/ 350°F/Gas Mark 4 for about 1 hour, or until the chicken is a rich golden brown, basting occasionally with the reserved lime and honey mixture.

5 When the chicken is cooked, boil the water from the roasting tin (pan) to reduce it to about 100 ml/3½ fl oz/scant ½ cup. Blend the cornflour (cornstarch) and water and stir into the reduced liquid. Heat gently to the boil, then stir until slightly thickened and clear. Serve the chicken with the sauce and stir-fried vegetables.

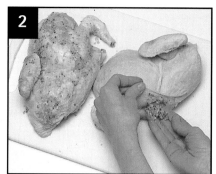

Chicken & Mango Stir-fry

A colourful, exotic mix of flavours that works surprisingly well,
this dish is easy and quick to cook – ideal for a mid-week family meal.

Serves 4

INGREDIENTS

6 boneless, skinless chicken thighs
2.5 cm/1 inch piece fresh ginger root,
  grated
1 garlic clove, crushed
1 small red chilli, deseeded
1 large red (bell) pepper

4 spring onions (scallions)
200 g/7 oz/1½ cups mangetout
  (snow peas)
100 g/3½ oz/1 cup baby sweetcorn
  (corn) cobs
1 large, firm, ripe mango

2 tbsp sunflower oil
1 tbsp light soy sauce
3 tbsp rice wine or sherry
1 tsp sesame oil
salt and pepper
sliced chives, to garnish

1 Cut the chicken into long, thin strips and place in a bowl. Mix together the ginger, garlic and chilli, then stir in to the chicken strips to coat them evenly.

2 Slice the (bell) pepper thinly, cutting diagonally. Trim and diagonally slice the spring onions (scallions). Cut the mangetouts (snow peas) and corn in half diagonally. Peel the mango, remove the stone (seed) and slice thinly.

3 Heat the oil in a large frying pan (skillet) or wok over a high heat. Add the chicken and stir-fry for 4–5 minutes until just turning golden brown. Add the (bell) peppers and stir-fry over a medium heat for 4–5 minutes to soften them.

4 Add the spring onions (scallions), mangetout (snow peas) and corn and stir-fry for a further minute.

5 Mix together the soy sauce, rice wine or sherry and sesame oil and stir it into the wok. Add the mango and stir gently for 1 minute to heat thoroughly.

6 Adjust the seasoning with salt and pepper to taste and serve immediately. Garnish with chives.

Thai-spiced Coriander Chicken

These simple marinated chicken breasts (halves) are packed with powerful, zesty flavours, and are best accompanied by a simple dish of plain boiled rice and a cucumber salad.

Serves 4

INGREDIENTS

4 boneless chicken breasts (halves), without skin
2 garlic cloves, peeled
1 fresh green chilli, deseeded
2 cm/¾ inch piece fresh ginger root, peeled

4 tbsp fresh coriander (cilantro), chopped
rind of 1 lime, finely grated
3 tbsp lime juice
2 tbsp light soy sauce
1 tbsp caster (superfine) sugar

175 ml/6 fl oz/¾ cup coconut milk
plain boiled rice, to serve
cucumber and radish slices, to garnish

1 Using a sharp knife, cut 3 deep slashes into the skinned side of each chicken breast (half). Place the breasts (halves) in a single layer in a wide, non-metallic dish.

2 Put the garlic, chilli, ginger, coriander (cilantro), lime rind and juice, soy sauce, caster (superfine) sugar and coconut milk in a food processor and process until a smooth purée forms.

3 Spread the purée over both sides of the chicken breasts (halves), coating them evenly. Cover the dish and leave to marinate in the refrigerator for about 1 hour.

4 Lift the chicken from the marinade, drain off the excess and place in a grill (broiler) pan. Grill (broil) under a preheated grill (broiler) for 12–15 minutes until thoroughly and evenly cooked.

5 Meanwhile, place the remaining marinade in a saucepan and bring to the boil. Lower the heat and simmer for several minutes to heat thoroughly. Serve with the chicken breasts, accompanied with rice and garnished with cucumber and radish slices.

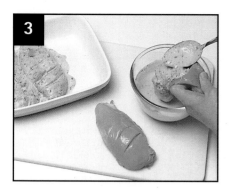

Green Chicken Curry

Thai curries are traditionally very hot, and designed to make a little go a long way – the thin, highly spiced juices are eaten with lots of rice to 'stretch' a small amount of meat as far as possible.

Serves 4

INGREDIENTS

6 boneless, skinless chicken thighs
400 ml/14 fl oz/1¾ cups coconut milk
2 garlic cloves, crushed
2 tbsp Thai fish sauce

2 tbsp Thai green curry paste
12 baby aubergines (eggplants), also
  called Thai pea aubergines
3 green chillies, finely chopped

3 kaffir lime leaves, shredded
4 tbsp fresh coriander (cilantro),
  chopped
boiled rice, to serve

1 Cut the chicken into bite-sized pieces. Pour the coconut milk into a large pan or wok over a high heat and bring to the boil.

2 Add the chicken, garlic and fish sauce to the pan and bring back to the boil. Lower the heat and simmer gently for 30 minutes, or until the chicken is just tender.

3 Remove the chicken from the mixture with a perforated spoon. Set aside and keep warm.

4 Stir the green curry paste into the pan, add the aubergines (eggplants), chillies and lime leaves and simmer for 5 minutes.

5 Return the chicken to the pan and bring to the boil. Adjust the seasoning to taste with salt and pepper, then stir in the coriander (cilantro). Serve the curry with boiled rice.

COOK'S TIP

Baby aubergines (eggplants), or 'pea aubergines' as they are called in Thailand, are traditionally used in this curry, but they are not always easily available outside the country. If you can't find them in an Oriental food shop, use chopped ordinary aubergine (eggplant) or substitute a few green peas.

Braised Chicken with Garlic & Spices

The intense flavours of this dish are helped by the slow, gentle cooking. The meat should be almost falling off the bone, virtually 'melting' into the velvety-smooth, spicy sauce.

Serves 4

INGREDIENTS

4 garlic cloves, chopped
4 shallots, chopped
2 small red chillies, deseeded and
    chopped
1 lemon grass stalk (stem), finely
    chopped
1 tbsp fresh coriander (cilantro),
    chopped

1 tsp shrimp paste
½ tsp ground cinnamon
1 tbsp tamarind paste
2 tbsp vegetable oil
8 small chicken joints, such as
    drumsticks or thighs
300 ml/10 fl oz/1¼ cups chicken
    stock

1 tbsp Thai fish sauce
1 tbsp smooth peanut butter
salt and pepper
4 tbsp toasted peanuts, chopped
stir-fried vegetables and boiled
    noodles, to serve

1 Place the garlic, shallots, chillies, lemon grass, coriander (cilantro) and shrimp paste in a pestle and mortar and grind to an almost smooth paste. Add the cinnamon and tamarind paste to the mixture.

2 Heat the oil in a wok a wide frying pan (skillet) or wok. Add the chicken joints, turning often, until they are golden brown on all sides. Remove them from the wok and keep hot. Tip away any excess fat.

3 Add the spice paste to the pan or wok and stir over a medium heat until lightly browned. Stir in the stock and return the chicken to the pan.

4 Bring to the boil, then cover tightly, lower the heat and simmer for 25–30 minutes, stirring occasionally, until the chicken is tender and thoroughly cooked. Stir in the fish sauce and peanut butter and simmer the mixture gently for a further 10 minutes.

5 Adjust the seasoning with salt and pepper to taste and scatter the toasted peanuts over the chicken. Serve hot, with colourful stir-fry vegetables and noodles.

Duck Breasts with Chilli & Lime

Duck is excellent cooked with strong flavours, and when it is marinated and coated in this rich, dark, sticky Oriental glaze it's irresistible. Serve with jasmine rice and a salad.

Serves 4

INGREDIENTS

4 boneless duck breasts (halves)
2 garlic cloves, crushed
4 tsp light soft brown sugar
3 tbsp lime juice

1 tbsp soy sauce
1 tsp chilli sauce
1 tsp vegetable oil
2 tbsp plum jam

120 ml/4 fl oz/½ cup chicken stock
salt and pepper

1 Using a small, sharp knife, cut deep slashes in the skin of the duck to make a diamond pattern. Place the duck breasts in a wide, non-metallic dish.

2 Mix together the garlic, sugar, lime juice, soy and chilli sauces, then spoon over the duck breasts (halves), turning well to coat them evenly. Cover the dish with cling film (plastic wrap) and leave to marinate in the refrigerator for at least 3 hours, or overnight.

3 Drain the duck, reserving the marinade. Heat a large, heavy-based pan until very hot and brush with the oil. Add the duck breasts, skin side down, and cook for about 5 minutes or until the skin is browned and crisp. Tip away the excess fat. Turn the duck breasts over.

4 Continue cooking on the other side for 2–3 minutes to brown. Add the reserved marinade, plum jam and stock and simmer for 2 minutes. Adjust the

seasoning to taste and serve hot, with the juices spooned over.

COOK'S TIP

If you prefer to reduce the overall fat content of this dish, remove the skin from the duck breasts (halves) before cooking and reduce the cooking time slightly.

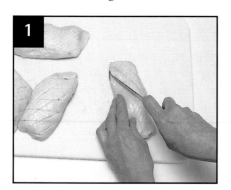

Roasted Duck Curried with Pineapple & Coconut

Duck is a fatty meat, but it has lots of rich flavour. In this recipe, the duck is 'roasted' under a hot grill (broiler) until golden brown and crispy, so much of the fat drains off before adding the meat to the curry.

Serves 4

INGREDIENTS

1.6 kg/3½ lb duckling
2 tbsp groundnut oil
1 small pineapple
1 large onion, chopped
1 garlic clove, finely chopped

1 tsp fresh ginger root, finely chopped
½ tsp ground coriander
1 tbsp Thai green curry paste
1 tsp soft light brown sugar
450 ml/16 fl oz/2 cups coconut milk

salt and pepper
fresh coriander (cilantro), chopped
red chilli strips, to garnish
boiled jasmine rice, to serve

1 Using a large knife or poultry shears, cut the duck in half lengthways, cutting through the line of the breastbone. Wipe inside and out with paper towels. Sprinkle with salt and pepper, prick the skin with a fork and brush with oil.

2 Place the duck, cut side down, on a grill (broiler) pan and grill (broil) under a preheated hot grill (broiler) for 25–30 minutes, turning occasionally, until golden brown. Tip away the fat in the pan, as it may burn.

3 Allow the duck to cool, then cut each half into 2 portions. Peel and core the pineapple, then cut the flesh into dice shapes.

4 Heat the remaining oil in a large pan and fry the onion and garlic for 3-4 minutes until softened. Stir in the ginger, ground coriander, curry paste and brown sugar and stir-fry for 1 minute.

5 Stir in the coconut milk and bring to the boil. Add the duck pieces and the pineapple. Reduce the heat and simmer for 5 minutes. Sprinkle with coriander (cilantro) and serve over boiled jasmine rice.

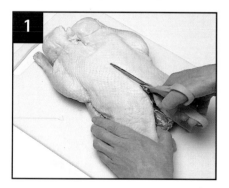
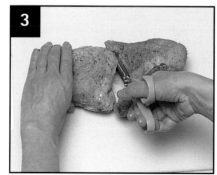

Steamed Yellow Fish Fillets

Thailand has an abundance of fresh fish, which is an important part of the local diet. Dishes such as these steamed fillets are popular and can be adapted to suit many different types of fish. Serve with a vegetable and beansprout salad.

Serves 4

INGREDIENTS

500 g/1 lb 2 oz firm fish fillets, such as red snapper, sole or monkfish
1 dried red bird-eye chilli
1 small onion, chopped
3 garlic cloves, chopped

2 sprigs fresh coriander (cilantro)
1 tsp coriander seeds
½ tsp turmeric
½ tsp ground black pepper
1 tbsp Thai fish sauce

2 tbsp coconut milk
1 small egg, beaten
2 tbsp rice flour
red and green chilli strips, to garnish
soy sauce, to serve

1 Remove any skin from the fish and cut the fillets diagonally into long 2 cm/¾ inch wide strips.

2 Place the dried chilli, onion, garlic, coriander (cilantro) and coriander seeds in a pestle and mortar and grind until it is a smooth paste.

3 Add the turmeric, pepper, fish sauce, coconut milk and beaten egg, stirring well to mix evenly.

4 Dip the fish strips into the paste mixture, then into the rice flour to coat lightly.

5 Bring the water in the bottom of a steamer to the boil, then arrange the fish strips in the top of the steamer. Cover and steam for about 12–15 minutes until the fish is just firm.

6 Serve the fish with soy sauce and an accompaniment of stir-fried vegetables or salad.

COOK'S TIP

If you don't have a steamer, improvise by placing a large metal colander over a large pan of boiling water and cover with an upturned plate to enclose the fish as it steams.

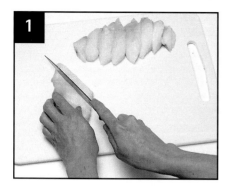

Baked Fish with Pepper, Chillies & Basil

Almost any whole fish can be cooked by this method, but snapper, sea bass or John Dory are particularly good with the Thai flavours.

Serves 4

INGREDIENTS

handful of fresh sweet basil leaves
750 g/1 lb 10 oz whole red snapper, sea bass or John Dory, cleaned
2 tbsp groundnut oil
2 tbsp Thai fish sauce
2 garlic cloves, crushed

1 tsp galangal or ginger root, finely grated
2 large fresh red chillies, sliced diagonally
1 yellow (bell) pepper, deseeded and diced

1 tbsp palm sugar
1 tbsp rice vinegar
2 tbsp water or fish stock
2 tomatoes, deseeded and sliced into thin wedges

1 Reserve a few fresh basil leaves for garnish and tuck the rest inside the body cavity of the fish.

2 Heat 1 tablespoon oil in a wide frying pan (skillet) and fry the fish quickly to brown, turning once. Place the fish on a large piece of foil in a roasting tin (pan) and spoon over the fish sauce. Wrap the foil over the fish loosely and bake in an oven preheated to 190°C/375°F/Gas Mark 5 for 25–30 minutes until just cooked though.

3 Meanwhile, heat the remaining oil and fry the garlic, galangal and chillies for 30 seconds. Add the pepper and stir-fry for a further 2–3 minutes to soften.

4 Stir in the sugar, rice vinegar and water, then add the tomatoes and bring to the boil. Remove the pan from the heat.

5 Remove the fish from the oven and transfer to a warmed serving plate. Add the fish juices to the pan, then spoon the sauce over the fish and scatter with the reserved basil leaves. Serve immediately.

COOK'S TIP

Large red chillies are less hot than the tiny red bird-eye chillies, so you can use them more freely in cooked dishes such as this for a mild heat. Remove the seeds if you prefer.

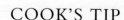

Baked Cod with a Curry Crust

An easy, economical main dish that transforms a plain piece of fish into an exotic meal – try it with other white fish, too, such as monkfish or halibut. Serve this with new potatoes and salad.

Serves 4

INGREDIENTS

½ tsp sesame oil

4 pieces cod fillet, about 150 g/5½ oz each

80 g/3 oz/1½ cups fresh white breadcrumbs

2 tbsp blanched almonds, chopped

2 tsp Thai green curry paste

rind of ½ lime, finely grated

salt and pepper

boiled new potatoes, to serve

lime slices and rind and mixed green leaves, to garnish

1 Brush the sesame oil over the base of a wide, shallow oven-proof dish or tin (pan), then place the pieces of cod in a single layer.

2 Mix the fresh breadcrumbs, almonds, curry paste and grated lime rind together, stirring well to blend thoroughly and evenly. Season to taste with salt and pepper.

3 Carefully spoon the crumb mixture over the fish pieces, pressing lightly to hold it in place.

4 Place the dish, uncovered, in a preheated oven at 200°C/400°F/Gas Mark 6 and bake for 35–40 minutes until the fish is cooked through and the crumb topping is golden brown.

5 Serve the dish hot, garnished with lime slices and rind and mixed green leaves and accompanied with boiled new potatoes.

COOK'S TIP

To test whether the fish is cooked through, use a fork to pierce it in the thickest part – if the flesh is white all the way through and flakes apart easily, it is cooked sufficiently.

Whole Fried Fish with Soy & Ginger

This impressive dish is worth cooking for a special dinner, as it really is a talking point.
Buy a very fresh whole fish on the day you plan to cook it, and ask your fishmonger to clean it,
preferably leaving the head on.

Serves 4–6

INGREDIENTS

6 dried Chinese mushrooms
3 tbsp rice vinegar
2 tbsp soft light brown sugar
3 tbsp dark soy sauce
7.5 cm/3 inch piece fresh ginger root,
   finely chopped

4 spring onions (scallions), sliced
   diagonally
2 tsp cornflour (cornstarch)
2 tbsp lime juice
1 sea bass, about 1 kg/2 lb 4 oz,
   cleaned

4 tbsp plain (all-purpose) flour
sunflower oil for deep frying
salt and pepper
shredded Chinese leaves and radish
   slices, to serve
1 radish, sliced but left whole, to garnish

1 Soak the dried mushrooms in hot water for about 10 minutes, then drain well, reserving 100 ml/3½ fl oz/scant ½ cup of the liquid. Cut the mushrooms into thin slices.

2 Mix the reserved mushroom liquid with the rice vinegar, sugar and soy sauce. Place in a saucepan with the mushrooms and bring to the boil. Reduce the heat and simmer for 3–4 minutes.

3 Add the ginger and spring onions (scallions) and simmer for 1 minute. Blend the cornflour (cornstarch) and lime juice together, stir into the pan and stir for 1–2 minutes until the sauce thickens and clears. Keep the sauce to one side while you cook the fish.

4 Season the fish inside and out with salt and pepper, then dust lightly with flour, carefully shaking off the excess.

5 Heat a 2.5 cm/1 inch depth of oil in a wide pan to 190°C/ 375°F or until a cube of bread browns in 30 seconds. Carefully lower the fish into the oil and fry on one side for about 3–4 minutes until golden. Use 2 metal spatulas or fish slices (pancake turners) to turn the fish carefully and fry on the other side for a further 3–4 minutes until golden brown.

6 Lift the fish out of the pan, draining off the excess oil, and place on a serving plate. Heat the sauce until boiling, then spoon it over the fish. Serve immediately, surrounded by shredded Chinese leaves with sliced radishes and garnished with the sliced whole radish.

Spiced Tuna in Sweet-and-Sour Sauce

Tuna is a firm, meaty-textured fish that is abundant in the seas around Thailand.
You can also use shark or mackerel with this rich sweet-and-sour sauce.

Serves 4

INGREDIENTS

4 fresh tuna steaks, about 500 g/
 1 lb 2 oz total weight
¼ tsp ground black pepper
2 tbsp groundnut oil
1 onion, diced
1 small red (bell) pepper, deseeded
 and cut into matchsticks
1 garlic clove, crushed

½ cucumber, deseeded and cut into
 matchsticks
2 pineapple slices, diced
1 tsp fresh ginger root, finely
 chopped
1 tbsp soft light brown sugar
1 tbsp cornflour (cornstarch)
1½ tbsp lime juice

1 tbsp Thai fish sauce
250 ml/9 fl oz/generous 1 cup fish
 stock
lime and cucumber slices,
 to garnish

1 Sprinkle the tuna steaks with pepper on both sides. Heat a heavy frying pan (skillet) or griddle and brush with a little of the oil. Arrange the tuna on the griddle and cook for about 8 minutes, turning them over once.

2 Heat the remaining oil in another pan and fry the onion, pepper and garlic gently for 3–4 minutes to soften.

3 Remove from the heat and stir in the cucumber, pineapple, ginger and sugar.

4 Blend the cornflour (cornstarch) with the lime juice and fish sauce, then stir into the stock and add to the pan. Stir over a medium heat until boiling, then cook for 1–2 minutes until thickened and clear.

5 Spoon the sauce over the tuna and serve garnished with lime slices and cucumber.

COOK'S TIP

Tuna can be served quite lightly cooked, and can be dry if it is overcooked.

Thai-spiced Salmon

Marinated in delicate Thai spices and quickly pan-fried to perfection, these salmon fillets are ideal for a special dinner. Serve them fresh from the pan to enjoy them at their best.

Serves 4

INGREDIENTS

2.5 cm/1 in piece fresh root ginger, grated
1 tsp coriander seeds, crushed
¼ tsp chilli powder

1 tbsp lime juice
1 tsp sesame oil
4 pieces salmon fillet with skin, about 150 g/5½ oz each

2 tbsp vegetable oil
boiled rice and stir-fried vegetables, to serve

1 Mix together the grated ginger, crushed coriander, chilli powder, lime juice and sesame oil.

2 Place the salmon on a wide, non-metallic plate or dish and spoon the mixture over the flesh side of the fillets, spreading it to coat each piece of salmon evenly.

3 Cover the dish with cling film (plastic wrap) and chill the salmon in the refrigerator for 30 minutes.

4 Heat a wide, heavy-based frying pan (skillet) or griddle pan with the oil over a high heat. Place the salmon on the hot pan or griddle, skin side down.

5 Cook the salmon for 4–5 minutes, without turning, until the salmon is crusty underneath and the flesh flakes easily. Serve at once with the boiled rice and stir-fried vegetables.

COOK'S TIP

It's important to use a heavy-based pan (skillet) or solid griddle for this recipe, so the fish cooks evenly throughout without sticking. If the fish is very thick, you may prefer to turn it over carefully to cook on the other side for 2–3 minutes.

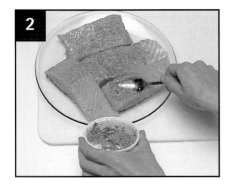

Salmon with Red Curry in Banana Leaves

Banana leaves are widely used in Thai cooking to wrap raw ingredients such as fish before baking or steaming. Oriental food shops usually stock them, but if you can't find any use foil or baking parchment.

Serves 4

INGREDIENTS

4 salmon steaks, about 175 g/6 oz
 each
2 banana leaves, halved
1 garlic clove, crushed
1 tsp fresh ginger root, grated

1 tbsp Thai red curry paste
1 tsp soft light brown sugar
1 tbsp Thai fish sauce
2 tbsp lime juice

TO GARNISH:
lime wedges
finely chopped red chilli

1 Place a salmon steak on the centre of each half banana leaf.

2 Mix together the garlic, ginger, curry paste, sugar and fish sauce. Spread this mixture over the surface of the fish and sprinkle with lime juice.

3 Wrap the banana leaves around the fish, tucking in the sides as you go to make a neat, compact bundle.

4 Place the parcels seam side down on a baking (cookie) sheet and bake in a preheated oven at 220°C/425°F/Gas Mark 7 for 15–20 minutes until the fish is cooked and the banana leaves are beginning to brown serve garnished with lime wedges and chilli.

COOK'S TIP

Fresh banana leaves are often sold in packs containing several leaves, but if you buy more than you need, they will store in the refrigerator for about a week.

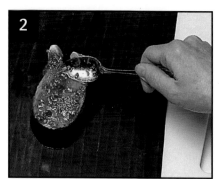

Spicy Thai Seafood Stew

The fish in this fragrant, curry-like stew can be varied according to taste or availability, but it's best to stick with those which stay firm when cooked, as delicate types will flake apart too easily.

Serves 4

INGREDIENTS

200 g/7 oz squid, cleaned

500 g/1 lb 2 oz firm white fish fillet, preferably monkfish or halibut

1 tbsp sunflower oil

4 shallots, finely chopped

2 garlic cloves, finely chopped

2 tbsp green Thai curry paste

2 small lemon grass stalks (stems), finely chopped

1 tsp shrimp paste

500 ml/18 fl oz/2¼ cups coconut milk

200 g/7 oz raw tiger prawns, peeled (shrimp), deveined

12 fresh clams in shells, cleaned

8 basil leaves, finely shredded

extra basil leaves, to garnish

boiled rice, to serve

1 Cut the squid body cavities into thick rings, and the fish into bite-sized chunks.

2 Heat the oil in a large frying pan (skillet) or wok and stir-fry the shallots, garlic and curry paste for 1–2 minutes. Add the lemon grass and shrimp paste, stir in the coconut milk and bring to the boil.

3 Reduce the heat until the liquid is simmering gently, then add the white fish, squid and prawns (shrimp) to the pan and simmer for 2 minutes.

4 Add the clams and simmer for a further minute until the clams open. Discard any clams that do not open.

5 Scatter the shredded basil leaves over the stew, and serve immediately, garnished with whole basil leaves and spooned over boiled rice.

COOK'S TIP

If you prefer, fresh mussels in shells can be used instead of clams – add them in Step 4 and follow the recipe.

Stir-fried Squid with Hot Black Bean Sauce

Quick stir-frying is an ideal cooking method for squid, as if overcooked it can be tough.
The technique also seals in the natural colours, flavours and nutritional value of fresh vegetables.

Serves 4

INGREDIENTS

750 g/1 lb 10 oz squid, cleaned
1 large red (bell) pepper, deseeded
80 g/3 oz/1 cup mangetout (snow peas), trimmed
1 head pak choi
3 tbsp black bean sauce

1 tbsp Thai fish sauce
1 tbsp rice wine
1 tbsp dark soy sauce
1 tsp soft light brown sugar
1 tsp cornflour (cornstarch)
1 tbsp water

1 tbsp sunflower oil
1 tsp sesame oil
1 small red bird eye chilli, chopped
1 garlic clove, finely chopped
1 tsp fresh ginger root, grated
2 spring onions (scallions), chopped

1 Cut the tentacles from the squid and discard. Cut the body cavities into quarters lengthways. Use the tip of a small sharp knife to score a diamond pattern into the flesh, without cutting all the way through. Pat dry with paper towels.

2 Cut the (bell) pepper into long, thin slices. Cut the mangetout (snow peas) in half diagonally. Coarsely shred the pak choi.

3 Mix together the black bean sauce, fish sauce, rice wine, soy sauce and sugar. Blend the cornflour (cornstarch) with the water and stir into the other sauce ingredients. Keep to one side.

4 Heat the oils in a wok. Add the chilli, garlic, ginger and spring onions (scallions) and stir-fry for about 1 minute. Add the (bell) pepper and stir-fry for about 2 minutes.

5 Add the squid and stir-fry over a high heat for a further minute. Stir in the mangetout (snowpeas) and pak choi, and stir for a further minute until wilted.

6 Stir in the sauce ingredients and cook, stirring, for about 2 minutes, until the sauce clears and thickens. Serve immediately.

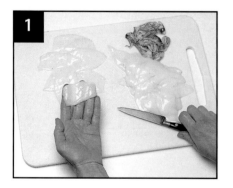

Spicy Scallops with Lime & Chilli

Really fresh scallops have a delicate flavour and texture, needing only minimal cooking, as in this simple stir-fry.

Serves 4

INGREDIENTS

16 large scallops
15 g/½ oz/1 tbsp butter
1 tbsp vegetable oil
1 tsp garlic, crushed
1 tsp fresh ginger root, grated

1 bunch spring onions (scallions), finely sliced
rind of 1 kaffir lime, finely grated
1 small red chilli, deseeded and very finely chopped

3 tbsp kaffir lime juice
salt and pepper
lime wedges and boiled rice, to serve

1 Trim the scallops to remove any black intestine, then wash and pat dry. Separate the corals from the white parts, then horizontally slice each white part in half, making 2 rounds.

2 Heat the butter and oil in a frying pan (skillet) or wok. Add the garlic and ginger and stir-fry for 1 minute without browning. Add the spring onions (scallions) and stir-fry for a further minute.

3 Add the scallops and continue stir-frying over a high heat for 4–5 minutes. Stir in the lime rind, chilli and lime juice and cook for a further minute.

4 Serve the scallops hot, with the juices spooned over them, accompanied by lime wedges and boiled rice.

COOK'S TIP

If fresh scallops are not available, frozen ones can be used, but make sure they are thoroughly defrosted before you cook them. Drain off all excess moisture and pat dry with paper towels.

Prawn Skewers with Chilli & Tamarind Glaze

Whole tiger prawns (shrimp) cook very quickly on a barbecue or under a grill (broiler) so they're ideal for summertime cooking, indoors or outside. All you need is a fresh salad and the meal is complete.

Serves 4

INGREDIENTS

1 garlic clove, chopped
1 red bird-eye chilli, deseeded and
  chopped
1 tbsp tamarind paste

1 tbsp sesame oil
1 tbsp dark soy sauce
2 tbsp lime juice
1 tbsp soft light brown sugar

16 large whole raw tiger prawns
  (shrimp)
crusty bread, lime wedges and salad
  leaves, to serve

1 Put the garlic, chilli, tamarind, sesame oil, soy sauce, lime juice and sugar in a small pan. Stir over a low heat until the sugar is dissolved, then remove from the heat and allow to cool completely.

2 Wash and dry the prawns (shrimp) and place in a single layer in a wide, non-metallic dish. Spoon the marinade over the prawns (shrimp) and turn them over to coat evenly. Cover the dish and leave in the refrigerator to marinate for at least 2 hours, or preferably overnight.

3 Meanwhile, soak 4 bamboo or wooden skewers in water for about 20 minutes. Drain and thread 4 prawns (shrimp) on to each skewer.

4 Grill (broil) the skewers under a preheated hot grill (broiler) for 5–6 minutes, turning them over once, until they turn pink and begin to brown. Alternatively, barbecue over hot coals.

5 Thread a wedge of lime on to the end of each skewer and serve with crusty bread and salad leaves.

Noodles & Rice

With its monsoon climate and abundant rainfall, Thailand has the ideal conditions for rice growing and has become one of the major rice producers in the world. It's thought that rice grew there as far back as 3500 BC. So, not surprisingly, rice is the main staple food in Thailand and hardly a meal goes by without it appearing in some form or another.

Two main varieties of rice are used in Thai cooking – a long and a short-grain. The long-grain is Thai fragrant rice, a good-quality white, fluffy rice with delicately scented, separate grains. Glutinous or 'sticky' rice is a round-grain rice with a high starch content which causes the grains to stick together.

Noodles also play a vital part in Thai meals, and street vendors serve them as a snack at all times of day. Rice noodles in flat ribbons (sticks) or thin vermicelli are the most common, and these need to be soaked before being fried or added to soups and stir-fries. Cellophane (mung bean) noodles are also locally made, but egg noodles are often imported from China. Most noodle dishes are served with an array of condiments for the diner to add to his or her taste – usually including crushed dried chillies, finely chopped peanuts, Thai fish sauce, soy sauce and sugar.

Crispy Rice Noodles

This is a version of a favourite Thai dish, 'mee krob', one of those exciting dishes which varies from one household to another and one day to the next – depending on the ingredients available.

Serves 4

INGREDIENTS

vegetable oil for deep frying, plus
  1½ tbsp
200 g/7 oz rice vermicelli noodles
1 onion, finely chopped
4 garlic cloves, finely chopped
1 boneless, skinless chicken breast
  (half), finely chopped
2 red bird-eye chillies, deseeded
  and sliced

4 tbsp dried black mushrooms, soaked
  and thinly sliced
3 tbsp dried prawns (shrimp)
4 spring onions (scallions), sliced
3 tbsp lime juice
2 tbsp soy sauce
2 tbsp Thai fish sauce
2 tbsp rice vinegar
2 tbsp soft light brown sugar

2 eggs, beaten
3 tbsp fresh coriander (cilantro),
  chopped
spring onion (scallion) curls,
  to garnish

1 Heat the oil in a large frying pan (skillet) or wok until very hot and deep-fry the noodles quickly, occasionally turning them, until puffed up, crisp and pale golden brown. Lift on to paper towels and drain well.

2 Heat 1 tablespoon oil and fry the onion and garlic for 1 minute. Add the chicken and stir-fry for 3 minutes. Add the chillies, mushrooms, dried prawns (shrimp) and spring onions (scallions).

3 Mix together the lime juice, soy sauce, fish sauce, rice vinegar and sugar, then stir into the pan and cook for a further minute. Remove the pan from the heat.

4 Heat the remaining oil in a wide pan and pour in the eggs to coat the base of the pan evenly, making a thin omelette. Cook until set and golden, then turn it over and cook the other side. Turn out and roll up, then slice into long ribbon strips.

5 Toss together the fried noodles, stir-fried ingredients, coriander (cilantro) and omelette strips. Garnish with spring onion (scallion) curls and serve at once.

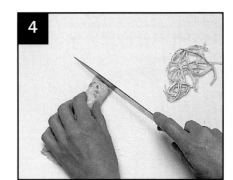

Sesame Noodles with Prawns & Coriander (cilantro)

*Delicately scented with sesame and coriander (cilantro),
these noodles make an unusual lunch or supper dish.*

Serves 4

INGREDIENTS

1 garlic clove, chopped
1 spring onion (scallion), chopped
1 small red chilli, deseeded and sliced
1 handful fresh coriander (cilantro)
300 g/10½ oz fine egg noodles

2 tbsp vegetable oil
2 tsp sesame oil
1 tsp shrimp paste
225 g/8 oz/1½ cups raw prawns
 (shrimp), peeled

2 tbsp lime juice
2 tbsp Thai fish sauce
1 tsp sesame seeds, toasted

1 Place the garlic, onion, chilli and coriander (cilantro) into a pestle and mortar and grind to a smooth paste.

2 Drop the noodles into a pan of boiling water and bring back to the boil, then simmer for 4 minutes, or according to the package directions.

3 Meanwhile, heat the oils in a pan and stir in the shrimp paste and ground coriander (cilantro) mixture. Stir over a medium heat for 1 minute.

4 Stir in the prawns (shrimp) and stir-fry for 2 minutes. Stir in the lime juice and fish sauce and cook for a further minute.

5 Drain the noodles and toss them into the wok. Sprinkle with the sesame seeds and serve.

COOK'S TIP

The roots of coriander (cilantro) are widely used in Thai cooking, so if you can buy fresh coriander (cilantro) with the root attached, the whole plant can be used in this dish for maximum flavour. If not, just use the stems and leaves.

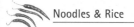

Hot & Sour Noodles

This simple, fast-food dish is sold from street food stalls in Thailand, with many and varied additions of meat and vegetables. It is equally good served hot or cold.

Serves 4

INGREDIENTS

250 g/9 oz dried medium egg noodles
1 tbsp sesame oil
1 tbsp chilli oil
1 garlic clove, crushed
2 spring onions (scallions), finely chopped

55 g/2 oz/²⁄₃ cup button mushrooms, sliced
40 g/1½ oz/1 cup dried Chinese black mushrooms, soaked, drained and sliced
2 tbsp lime juice

3 tbsp light soy sauce
1 tsp sugar

TO SERVE:
shredded Chinese leaves
2 tbsp shredded coriander (cilantro)
2 tbsp toasted peanuts, chopped

1 Cook the noodles in a large pan of boiling water for 3–4 minutes, or according to the package directions. Drain well, return to the pan, toss with the sesame oil and set aside.

2 Heat the chilli oil in a large frying pan (skillet) or wok and quickly stir-fry the garlic, onions and button mushrooms to soften them.

3 Add the black mushrooms, lime juice, soy sauce and sugar and continue stir-frying until boiling. Add the noodles and toss to mix.

4 Serve spooned over Chinese leaves, sprinkled with coriander (cilantro) and peanuts.

COOK'S TIP

Thai chilli oil is very hot, so if you want a milder flavour, use vegetable oil for the initial cooking instead, then add a final dribble of chilli oil just for seasoning.

Pad Thai Noodles

The combination of ingredients in this classic noodle dish varies, depending on the cook, but it commonly contains a mixture of pork and prawns or other seafood.

Serves 4

INGREDIENTS

250 g/9 oz rice stick noodles
3 tbsp groundnut oil
3 garlic cloves, finely chopped
125 g/4½ oz pork fillet (tenderloin), chopped into 5 mm/¼ inch pieces
200 g/7 oz/1¼ cups prawns (shrimp), peeled

1 tbsp sugar
3 tbsp Thai fish sauce
1 tbsp tomato ketchup
1 tbsp lime juice
2 eggs, beaten
125 g/4½ oz/generous 1 cup beansprouts

TO GARNISH:
1 tsp dried red chilli flakes
2 spring onions (scallions), thickly sliced
2 tbsp fresh coriander (cilantro), chopped

1 Soak the rice noodles in hot water for about 15 minutes, or according to the package directions. Drain well and put to one side.

2 Heat the oil in a large frying pan (skillet) or wok and fry the garlic over a high heat for 30 seconds. Add the pork and stir-fry for 2–3 minutes until browned.

3 Stir in the prawns (shrimp), then add the sugar, fish sauce, ketchup and lime juice, and continue stir-frying for a further 30 seconds.

4 Stir in the eggs and stir-fry until lightly set. Stir in the noodles, then add the beansprouts and stir-fry for a further 30 seconds to cook lightly.

5 Turn out on to a serving dish and scatter with chilli flakes, spring onions (scallions) and coriander (cilantro).

COOK'S TIP

Drain the rice noodles before adding to the pan, as excess moisture will spoil the texture of the dish.

Rice Noodles with Mushrooms & Tofu

An alternative to classic dishes such as Pad Thai Noodles (see page 134), this quick and easy dish is very filling. If you omit the fish sauce, it can be served as a vegetarian dish.

Serves 4

INGREDIENTS

225 g/8 oz rice stick noodles
2 tbsp vegetable oil
1 garlic clove, finely chopped
2 cm/¾ inch piece fresh ginger root, finely chopped
4 shallots, thinly sliced

70 g/2½ oz/¾ cup shiitake mushrooms, sliced
100 g/3½ oz/½ cup firm tofu, cut into 1.5 cm/⅝ inch dice
2 tbsp light soy sauce
1 tbsp rice wine

1 tbsp Thai fish sauce
1 tbsp smooth peanut butter
1 tsp chilli sauce
2 tbsp toasted peanuts, chopped
shredded basil leaves, to serve

1 Soak the rice stick noodles in hot water for 15 minutes, or according to the package directions. Drain well.

2 Heat the oil in a pan and stir-fry the garlic, ginger and shallots for 1–2 minutes until softened and lightly browned.

3 Add the mushrooms and stir-fry for a further 2–3 minutes. Stir in the tofu and toss gently to brown lightly.

4 Mix together the soy sauce, rice wine, fish sauce, peanut butter and fish sauce, then stir into the pan.

5 Stir in the rice noodles and toss to coat evenly in the sauce. Scatter with peanuts and shredded basil leaves and serve hot.

COOK'S TIP

For an easy storecupboard (pantry) dish, replace the shiitake mushrooms with a can of Chinese straw mushrooms. Alternatively, use dried shiitake mushrooms, soaked and drained before use.

Thai-style Noodle Rostis

Serve these crisp, fried 'rosti' noodle pancakes as an unusual first course,
or as a decorative side dish alongside meat dishes.

Serves 4

INGREDIENTS

125 g/4½ oz vermicelli rice noodles
2 spring onions (scallions), finely
   shredded
1 lemon grass stalk (stem), finely
   shredded
3 tbsp fresh coconut, finely shredded

salt and pepper
vegetable oil for frying

TO SERVE:
115 g/4 oz/generous 1 cup
   beansprouts

1 small red onion, thinly sliced
1 avocado, thinly sliced
2 tbsp lime juice
2 tbsp rice wine
1 tsp chilli sauce
whole red chillies, to garnish

1 Break the rice noodles into short pieces and soak in hot water for about 4 minutes, or according to package directions. Drain thoroughly and pat dry with paper towels.

2 Stir together the noodles, spring onions (scallions), lemon grass and coconut.

3 Heat a small amount of oil until very hot in a heavy-based frying pan (skillet). Brush a 9 cm/3½ inch round biscuit (cookie) cutter with oil and place in the pan. Spoon a small amount of noodle mixture into the cutter to just cover the base of the pan, then press down lightly with the back of a spoon.

4 Fry for 30 seconds, then carefully remove the cutter and continue frying the rosti until it is golden brown, turning it over once. Remove and drain on paper towels. Repeat with the remaining noodles, to make about 12 rostis.

5 To serve, arrange the noodle rostis in small stacks, with beansprouts, onion and avocado between the layers. Mix the lime juice, rice wine and chilli sauce together and spoon over just before serving, garnished with red chillies.

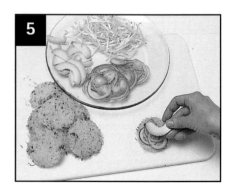

Drunken Noodles

Perhaps this would be more correctly named 'drunkards' noodles', as it's a dish that is supposedly often eaten as a hangover cure – the fiery kick of the chillies wakes up the system and the lime leaves and basil cleanse and refresh the palate.

Serves 4

INGREDIENTS

175 g/6 oz rice stick noodles
2 tbsp vegetable oil
1 garlic clove, crushed
2 small green chillies, chopped
1 small onion, thinly sliced
150 g/5½ oz lean minced (ground)
   pork or chicken

1 small green (bell) pepper, deseeded
   and finely chopped
4 kaffir lime leaves, finely shredded
1 tbsp dark soy sauce
1 tbsp light soy sauce
½ tsp sugar
1 tomato, cut into thin wedges

2 tbsp sweet basil leaves, finely sliced,
   to garnish

1 Soak the rice stick noodles in hot water for 15 minutes, or according to the package directions. Drain well.

2 Heat the oil in a wok and stir-fry the garlic, chillies and onion for 1 minute.

3 Stir in the pork or chicken and stir-fry on a high heat for a further minute, then add the pepper and continue stir-frying for a further 2 minutes.

4 Stir in the lime leaves, soy sauces and sugar. Add the noodles and tomato and toss well to heat thoroughly.

5 Sprinkle with the sliced basil leaves and serve hot.

COOK'S TIP

Fresh kaffir lime leaves freeze well, so if you buy more than you need, simply tie them in a tightly sealed polythene (plastic) freezer bag and freeze for up to a month. They can be used straight from the freezer.

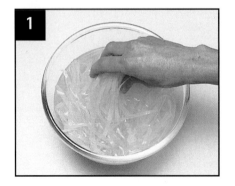

Crispy Duck with Noodles & Tamarind

A robustly flavoured dish that makes a substantial main course.
Serve it with a refreshing cucumber salad or a light vegetable stir-fry.

Serves 4

INGREDIENTS

3 duck breasts (halves), total weight
    about 400 g/14 oz
2 garlic cloves, crushed
1½ tsp chilli paste
1 tbsp honey

3 tbsp dark soy sauce
½ tsp five-spice powder
250 g/9 oz rice stick noodles
1 tsp vegetable oil
1 tsp sesame oil

2 spring onion (scallions), sliced
100 g/3½ oz mangetout (snow peas)
2 tbsp tamarind juice
sesame seeds, to garnish

1 Prick the duck breast skin all over with a fork and place in a deep dish.

2 Mix together the garlic, chilli, honey, soy sauce and five-spice powder, then pour over the duck. Turn the breasts (halves) over to coat them evenly, then cover and leave to marinate in the refrigerator for at least 1 hour.

3 Meanwhile, soak the rice noodles in hot water for 15 minutes. Drain well.

4 Drain the duck breasts halves from the marinade and grill (broil) on a rack under high heat for about 10 minutes, turning them over occasionally, until they become a rich golden brown. Remove and slice the duck breasts (halves) thinly.

5 Heat the vegetable and sesame oils in a pan and toss the spring onions (scallions) and mangetout (snow peas) for 2 minutes. Stir in the reserved marinade and tamarind and bring to the boil.

6 Add the sliced duck and noodles and toss to heat thoroughly. Serve immediately, sprinkled with sesame seeds.

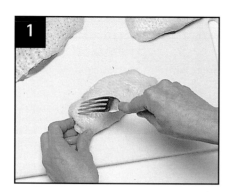

Rice Noodles with Chicken & Chinese Leaves

The great thing about stir-fries is you can cook with very little fat and still get lots of flavour, as in this light, healthy lunch dish that's low in fat and very quick to make.

Serves 4

INGREDIENTS

200 g/7 oz rice stick noodles
1 tbsp sunflower oil
1 garlic clove, finely chopped
2 cm/¾ inch piece fresh ginger root, finely chopped
4 spring onions (scallions), chopped
1 red bird-eye chilli, deseeded and sliced

300 g/10½ oz/2 cups boneless, skinless chicken, finely chopped
2 chicken livers, finely chopped
1 celery stick, thinly sliced
1 carrot, cut into fine matchsticks
300 g/10½ oz/5½ cups shredded Chinese leaves
4 tbsp lime juice

2 tbsp Thai fish sauce
1 tbsp soy sauce

TO GARNISH:
2 tbsp fresh mint, shredded
slices of pickled garlic
fresh mint sprig

1 Soak the rice noodles in hot water for 15 minutes, or according to the package directions. Drain well.

2 Heat the oil in a wok or large frying pan (skillet) and stir-fry the garlic, ginger, spring onions (scallions) and chilli for about 1 minute. Stir

in the chicken and chicken livers, then stir-fry over a high heat for 2–3 minutes until beginning to brown.

3 Stir in the celery and carrot and stir-fry for 2 minutes to soften. Add the Chinese leaves, then stir in the lime juice, fish sauce and soy sauce.

4 Add the noodles and stir to heat thoroughly. Sprinkle with shredded mint and pickled garlic. Serve immediately, garnished with a mint sprig.

Rice Noodles with Spinach

This quick stir-fried noodle dish is simple to prepare, and makes a delicious light lunch in minutes. You can leave out the dried prawns (shrimp), or replace them with chopped peanuts for a vegetarian dish.

Serves 4

INGREDIENTS

115 g/4 oz thin rice stick noodles
2 tbsp dried prawns (shrimp),
(optional)

250 g/9 oz/4 cups fresh young
spinach
1 tbsp groundnut oil
2 garlic cloves, finely chopped

2 tsp Thai green curry paste
1 tsp sugar
1 tbsp light soy sauce

1 Soak the noodles in hot water for 15 minutes, or according to the package directions, then drain well.

2 Soak the prawns (shrimp) in hot water for 10 minutes and drain well. Wash the spinach thoroughly, drain well and remove any tough stalks (stems).

3 Heat the oil in a large frying pan (skillet) or wok and stir-fry the garlic for 1 minute. Stir in the curry paste and stir-fry for 30 seconds. Stir in the soaked shrimp and stir-fry for 30 seconds.

4 Add the spinach and stir-fry for 1–2 minutes until the leaves are just wilted.

5 Stir in the sugar and soy sauce, then add the noodles and toss thoroughly to mix evenly. Serve immediately while hot.

COOK'S TIP

It is best to choose young spinach leaves for this dish, as they are beautifully tender and cook within a matter of seconds. If you can only get older spinach, however, shred the leaves before adding to the dish so they cook more quickly.

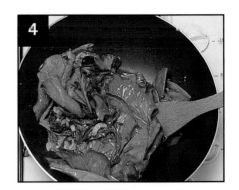

Egg Noodle Salad with Coconut, Lime & Basil Dressing

A good dish for summer eating, this is light and refreshing in flavour and easy to cook. The turkey can be replaced with cooked chicken if you prefer.

Serves 4

INGREDIENTS

225 g/8 oz dried egg noodles
2 tsp sesame oil
1 carrot
100 g/3½ oz/1 cup beansprouts
½ cucumber
150 g/5½ oz cooked turkey breast meat, shredded into thin slivers

2 spring onions (scallions), finely shredded
peanuts and basil leaves chopped, to garnish

DRESSING:
5 tbsp coconut milk

3 tbsp lime juice
1 tbsp light soy sauce
2 tsp Thai fish sauce
1 tsp chilli oil
1 tsp sugar
2 tbsp coriander (cilantro), chopped
2 tbsp sweet basil, chopped

1 Cook the noodles in boiling water for 4 minutes, or according to the package directions. Plunge them into a bowl of cold water to cool, then drain and toss in sesame oil.

2 Use a vegetable peeler to shave off thin ribbons from the carrot. Blanch the ribbons and beansprouts in boiling water for 30 seconds, then plunge into cold water for 30 seconds. Drain well. Next, shave thin ribbons of cucumber with the peeler.

3 Toss the carrots, beansprouts, cucumber and spring onions (scallions) together with the turkey and noodles.

4 Place the dressing ingredients in a screw-top jar and shake well to mix evenly.

5 Add the dressing to the noodle mixture and toss. Pile on to a serving dish. Sprinkle with peanuts and basil. Serve cold.

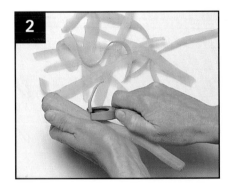

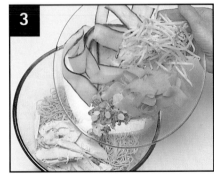

Stir-fried Rice with Egg Strips

Many Thai rice dishes are made from leftover rice that has been cooked for an earlier meal. But nothing goes to waste, and it's often stir-fried with a few simple ingredients and aromatic flavourings, as in this recipe. If you have any leftover vegetables or meat, this is a good way to use them up.

Serves 4

INGREDIENTS

2 tbsp groundnut oil
1 egg, beaten with 1 tsp water
1 garlic clove, finely chopped
1 small onion, finely chopped
1 tbsp Thai red curry paste
250 g/9 oz/2 cups long-grain rice, cooked

55 g/2 oz/⅓ cup cooked peas
1 tbsp Thai fish sauce
2 tbsp tomato ketchup
2 tbsp fresh coriander (cilantro), chopped

TO GARNISH:
red chillies
cucumber slices

1 To make chilli flowers, hold the stem with your fingertips and use a small sharp, pointed knife to cut a slit down the length from near the stem end to the tip. Turn the chilli about a quarter turn and make another cut. Repeat to make a total of 4 cuts, then scrape out the seeds. Cut each 'petal' again in half, or into quarters, to make 8–16 petals. Place the chilli in iced water.

2 Heat about 1 teaspoon of the oil in a wok. Pour in the egg mixture, swirling it to coat the pan evenly and make a thin layer. When set and golden, remove the egg from the pan and roll up. Keep to one side.

3 Add the remaining oil to the pan and stir-fry the garlic and onion for 1 minute. Add the curry paste, then stir in the rice and peas.

4 Stir in the fish sauce and ketchup. Remove the pan from the heat and pile the rice on to a serving dish.

5 Slice the egg roll into spiral strips, without unrolling, and use to garnish the rice. Add the cucumber slices and chilli flowers. Serve hot.

Jasmine Rice
with Lemon & Basil

*Jasmine rice has a delicate flavour and it can be served completely plain, with no other flavourings.
This simple dish just has the light tang of lemon and soft scent of basil to add an extra touch.*

Serves 4

INGREDIENTS

400 g/14 oz/2 cups jasmine rice
800 ml/28 fl oz/3½ cups water

rind of ½ lemon, finely grated

2 tbsp fresh sweet basil, chopped

1 Wash the rice in several changes of cold water until the water runs clear. Bring the water to the boil in a large pan, then add the rice.

2 Bring back to a rolling boil. Turn the heat to a low simmer, cover the pan and simmer for a further 12 minutes.

3 Remove the pan from the heat and leave to stand, covered, for 10 minutes.

4 Fluff up the rice with a fork, then stir in the lemon. Serve scattered with basil.

COOK'S TIP

It is important to leave the pan tightly covered while the rice cooks and steams inside so the grains cook evenly and become fluffy and separate.

Rice with Seafood

This soup-like main course rice dish is packed with fresh seafood, typically Thai in flavour.
If you have time, make your own fish stock from fish trimmings, or use good quality stock cubes.

Serves 4

INGREDIENTS

12 mussels in shells, cleaned
2 litres/3½ pints/8¾ cups fish stock
2 tbsp vegetable oil
1 garlic clove, crushed
1 tsp fresh ginger root, grated
1 red bird-eye chilli, chopped
2 spring onions (scallions), chopped

225 g/8 oz/scant 1¼ cups
  long-grain rice
2 small squid, cleaned and sliced
100 g/3½ oz firm white fish fillet,
  such as halibut or monkfish, cut
  into chunks

100 g/3½ oz raw prawns (shrimp),
  peeled
2 tbsp Thai fish sauce
3 tbsp fresh coriander (cilantro),
  shredded

1 Discard any mussels with damaged shells or open ones that do not close when firmly tapped. Heat 4 tablespoons of the stock in a large pan. Add the mussels, cover and shake the pan until the mussels open. Remove from the heat and discard any which do not open.

2 Heat the oil in a large frying pan (skillet) or wok and fry the garlic, ginger, chilli and spring onions (scallions) for 30 seconds. Add the stock and bring to the boil.

3 Stir in the rice, then add the squid, fish fillet and prawns (shrimp). Lower the heat and simmer gently for 15 minutes, or until the rice is cooked. Add the fish sauce and mussels.

4 Ladle into wide bowls and sprinkle with coriander (cilantro), before serving.

COOK'S TIP

You could use leftover cooked rice for this dish. Just simmer the seafood gently until cooked, then stir in the rice at the end.

Coconut Rice with Pineapple

Cooking rice in coconut milk makes it very satisfying and nutritious, and this is often used as a base for main dishes, with the addition of meat, fish, vegetables or eggs to make it more substantial.

Serves 4

INGREDIENTS

200 g/7 oz/1 cup long-grain rice
500 ml/18 fl oz/2¼ cups coconut milk
2 lemon grass stalks (stems)

200 ml/7 fl oz/scant 1 cup water
2 slices fresh pineapple, peeled and
diced

2 tbsp toasted coconut
chilli sauce, to serve

1 Wash the rice in several changes of cold water until the water runs clear. Place in a large pan with the coconut milk.

2 Place the lemon grass on a firm work surface and bruise it by hitting firmly with a rolling pin or meat hammer. Add to the pan with the rice and coconut milk.

3 Add the water and bring to the boil. Lower the heat, cover the pan tightly and simmer gently for 15 minutes. Remove the pan from the heat and fluff up the rice with a fork.

4 Remove the lemon grass and stir in the pineapple. Scatter with toasted coconut and serve with chilli sauce.

VARIATION

A sweet version of this dish can be made by simply omitting the lemon grass and stirring in palm sugar or caster sugar to taste during cooking. Serve as a dessert, with extra pineapple slices.

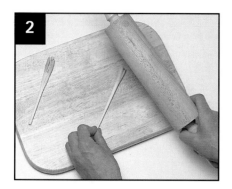

Vegetables & Salads

Many of the local vegetables, salad leaves and shoots which Thais use in vegetable dishes and salads are native, often growing wild locally and are uncultivated. This makes it difficult to produce really authentic Thai salads at home, as even the best Oriental food stores can not source all the fresh ingredients.

You may be reduced to substituting a few fresh ingredients with canned ones, or local Thai vegetables with more familiar Western ones, but luckily you can now buy a good selection of cultivated Oriental vegetables such as pak choi and Chinese leaves. So, with a few careful choices, it's easy to produce some imaginative vegetable dishes with distinctly Thai flavours.

A Thai salad can make a stunning centrepiece for any dinner table. Thai cooks usually add strips of finely chopped cooked meat, fish or shellfish to their salads, or for vegetarian dishes, mushrooms or tofu will appear.

Dressings are typically piquant and spicy, with the usual skillful balance of bitter, salt, sour, hot and sweet tastes. To finish, a sprinkling of crushed peanuts or dried chillies, chopped coriander (cilantro) or mint, slices of pickled garlic, and a final flourish of chilli flowers or spring onion (scallion) tassels will add colour to the dish.

Crisp Pickled Vegetables

These crisp, delicately preserved vegetables are usually served as an accompaniment to fried meat or fish dishes. Thai cooks love to cut vegetables decoratively, and would typically cut the carrots into small flower shapes, but if you're short of time, thin slices look just fine.

Serves 6–8

INGREDIENTS

½ small cauliflower
½ cucumber
2 carrots
200 g/7 oz French (green) beans

½ small Chinese cabbage
500 ml/18 fl oz/2¼ cups rice vinegar
1 tbsp caster (superfine) sugar
1 tsp salt

3 garlic cloves
3 shallots
3 red bird-eye chillies
5 tbsp groundnut oil

1 Trim the cauliflower. Peel and deseed the cucumber. Peel the carrots. Top and tail the beans. Trim the cabbage, then cut all the vegetables into bite-sized pieces. If you have time, cut the carrots into flower shapes.

2 Place the rice vinegar, sugar and salt in a large pan and bring almost to the boil. Add the vegetables, lower the heat and simmer for 3–4 minutes until they are just tender, but still crisp inside. Remove the pan from the heat and leave the vegetables and vinegar to cool.

3 Peel the garlic and shallots and deseed the chillies. Place in a pestle and mortar and grind until a smooth paste forms.

4 Heat the oil in a frying pan (skillet) and stir-fry the spice paste gently for 1–2 minutes. Add the vegetables with the vinegar and cook for a further 2 minutes to reduce the liquid slightly. Remove from the heat and leave to cool.

5 Serve the pickles cold, or pack into jars and store in the refrigerator for up to 2 weeks.

COOK'S TIP

To make simple carrot flowers, peel the carrot thinly as usual, then use a cannele knife or small sharp knife to cut narrow 'channels' down the length of it at regular intervals. Slice the carrot as usual and the slices will resemble flowers.

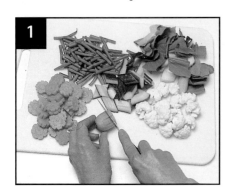

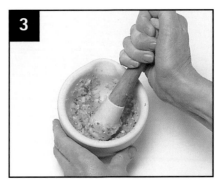

Chilli & Coconut Sambal

A sweet-sour sambal that goes well with grilled (broiled) or barbecued fish.
It can also be stirred into rice or noodles or curry dishes as extra flavouring.
Adjust the amount of chilli to your own taste.

Serves 6–8

INGREDIENTS

1 small coconut
1 slice fresh pineapple, finely diced
1 small onion, finely chopped
2 small green chillies, deseeded and
   chopped

5 cm/2 inch piece lemon grass
½ tsp salt
1 tsp shrimp paste
1 tbsp lime juice

2 tbsp fresh coriander (cilantro),
   chopped
coriander (cilantro) sprigs, to garnish

1 Puncture 2 of the coconut eyes with a screwdriver and pour the milk out from the shell. Crack the coconut shell, prise away the flesh and coarsely grate it into a bowl.

2 Mix the coconut with the pineapple, onion, chillies and lemon grass.

3 Blend together the salt, shrimp paste and lime juice, then stir into the sambal.

4 Stir in the coriander (cilantro). Spoon into a small dish to serve, and garnish with fresh coriander (cilantro) sprigs.

COOK'S TIP

The coconut can be grated quickly by using a grating blade on a food processor.

VARIATION

To make a quicker version of this sambal, stir a teaspoon of Thai green curry paste into freshly grated coconut and add finely diced pineapple and lime juice to taste.

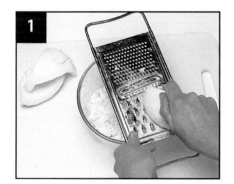

Mixed Vegetables in Peanut Sauce

This colourful mix of vegetables in a rich, spicy peanut sauce can be served either as a side dish or as a vegetarian main course.

Serves 4

INGREDIENTS

2 carrots, peeled
1 small head cauliflower, trimmed
2 small heads green pak choi
150 g/5½ oz French (green) beans, topped and tailed, if wished

2 tbsp vegetable oil
1 garlic clove, finely chopped
6 spring onions (scallions), sliced
1 tsp chilli paste

2 tbsp soy sauce
2 tbsp rice wine
4 tbsp smooth peanut butter
3 tbsp coconut milk

1 Cut the carrots diagonally into thin slices. Cut the cauliflower into small florets, then slice the stalk (stem) thinly. Thickly slice the pak choi. Cut the beans into 3 cm/1¼ inch lengths.

2 Heat the oil in a large frying pan (skillet) or wok and stir-fry the garlic and spring onions (scallions) for about 1 minute. Stir in the chilli paste and cook for a few seconds.

3 Add the carrots and cauliflower and stir-fry for 2–3 minutes.

4 Add the pak choi and beans and stir-fry for a further 2 minutes. Stir in the soy sauce and rice wine.

5 Mix the peanut butter with the coconut milk and stir into the pan, then cook, stirring, for a further minute. Serve immediately while still hot.

COOK'S TIP

It's important to cut the vegetables thinly into even-sized pieces so they cook quickly and evenly. Prepare all the vegetables before you start to cook.

Thai Red Bean Curry

The 'red' in the title refers not to the beans, but to the sauce, which has a warm, rusty red colour. This is a good way to serve fresh beans, and to lift the flavour of frozen beans, too.

Serves 4

INGREDIENTS

400 g/14 oz French (green) beans
1 garlic clove, finely sliced
1 red bird-eye chilli, deseeded and
    chopped

½ tsp paprika pepper
1 piece lemon grass stalk (stem),
    finely chopped
2 tsp Thai fish sauce

120 ml/4 fl oz/½ cup coconut milk
1 tbsp sunflower oil
2 spring onions (scallions), sliced

1 Cut the beans into 5 cm/ 2 inch pieces and cook in boiling water for about 2 minutes. Drain well.

2 Place the garlic, chilli, paprika, lemon grass, fish sauce and coconut milk in a blender and process until a smooth paste forms.

3 Heat the oil and stir-fry the spring onions (scallions) over a high heat for about 1 minute. Add the paste and bring the mixture to the boil.

4 Simmer for 3–4 minutes to reduce the liquid by about half. Add the beans and simmer for a further 1–2 minutes until tender. Serve hot.

COOK'S TIP

Young runner beans can be used instead of French (green) beans. Remove any strings from the beans, then cut at a diagonal angle in short lengths. Cook as the recipe until tender.

Stir-fried Ginger Mushrooms

*This quick vegetarian stir-fry is actually more like a rich curry,
with lots of warm spice and garlic, balanced with creamy coconut milk.*

Serves 4

INGREDIENTS

2 tbsp vegetable oil
3 garlic cloves, crushed
1 tbsp Thai red curry paste
½ tsp turmeric
425 g/14½ oz can Chinese straw
   mushrooms, drained and halved
2 cm/¾ inch piece fresh ginger root,
   finely shredded

100 ml/3½ fl oz/scant ½ cup
   coconut milk
40 g/1½ oz/1 cup dried Chinese
   black mushrooms, soaked, drained
   and sliced
1 tbsp lemon juice
1 tbsp light soy sauce
2 tsp sugar

8 cherry tomatoes, halved
200 g/7oz firm tofu, diced
½ tsp salt
coriander (cilantro) leaves, to garnish
boiled fragrant rice, to serve

1 Heat the oil and fry the garlic for about 1 minute, stirring. Stir in the curry paste and turmeric and cook for about a further 30 seconds.

2 Stir in the straw mushrooms and ginger and stir-fry for about 2 minutes. Stir in the coconut milk and bring to the boil.

3 Stir in the Chinese dried black mushrooms, lemon juice, soy sauce, sugar and salt and heat thoroughly. Add the tomatoes and tofu and toss gently to heat through.

4 Scatter the coriander (cilantro) over the mixture and serve hot, with fragrant rice.

COOK'S TIP

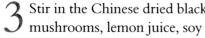

You can vary the mushrooms depending on your own taste – try a mixture of oyster and shiitake for a change – or even just ordinary cultivated button mushrooms are very tasty cooked this way.

Thai-spiced Mushrooms

An unusual dish that makes a good vegetarian main course.
Serve the mushrooms with a colourful fresh salad.

Serves 4

INGREDIENTS

8 large, flat mushrooms
3 tbsp sunflower oil
2 tbsp light soy sauce
1 garlic clove, crushed
2 cm/¾ inch piece fresh galangal or
   ginger root, grated

1 tbsp Thai green curry paste
8 baby sweetcorn (corn) cobs, sliced
3 spring onions (scallions), chopped
125 g/4½ oz/generous 1 cup
   beansprouts
100 g/3½ oz firm tofu, diced

2 tsp sesame seeds, toasted,

TO SERVE:
chopped cucumber
sliced red (bell) pepper

1 Remove the stalks (stems) from the mushrooms and set aside. Place the caps on a baking (cookie) sheet. Mix 2 tablespoons of the oil with 1 tablespoon of the light soy sauce and brush over the mushrooms.

2 Grill (broil) the mushroom caps under high heat until golden and tender, turning them over once.

3 Meanwhile, chop the mushroom stalks (stems) finely. Heat the remaining oil and stir-fry the stalks (stems) with the garlic and galangal or ginger for 1 minute.

4 Stir in the curry paste, baby sweetcorn (corn) and spring onions (scallions) and stir-fry for 1 minute. Add the beansprouts and stir for a further minute.

5 Add the tofu and remaining soy sauce, then toss lightly to heat. Spoon the mixture into the mushroom caps.

6 Sprinkle with the sesame seeds. Serve immediately with chopped cucumber and sliced red (bell) pepper.

COOK'S TIP

Galangal or ginger can be frozen for several weeks, either peeled and finely chopped ready to add to dishes, or in whole pieces. Thaw the piece or grate finely from frozen.

Oriental Vegetables with Yellow Bean Sauce

Serve this colourful mixture with a pile of golden, crispy noodles as a vegetarian main course, or on its own to accompany meat dishes.

Serves 4

INGREDIENTS

1 aubergine (eggplant)
salt
2 tbsp vegetable oil
3 garlic cloves, crushed
4 spring onions (scallions), chopped
1 small red (bell) pepper, deseeded
  and thinly sliced
4 baby sweetcorn, halved
  lengthways

80 g/3 oz/1 cup mangetout (snow
  peas)
200 g/7 oz/2 cups Chinese mustard
  greens, coarsely shredded
425 g/14½ oz can Chinese straw
  mushrooms, drained
125 g/4½ oz/generous 1 cup
  beansprouts
2 tbsp rice wine

2 tbsp yellow bean sauce
2 tbsp dark soy sauce
1 tsp chilli sauce
1 tsp sugar
125 ml/4 fl oz/½ cup chicken or
  vegetable stock
1 tsp cornflour (cornstarch)
2 tsp water

1 Trim the aubergine (eggplant) and cut into 5 cm/2 inch long matchsticks. Place in a colander, sprinkle with salt and leave to drain for 30 minutes. Rinse in cold water and dry with paper towels.

2 Heat the oil in a frying pan (skillet) or wok and stir-fry the garlic, spring onions (scallions) and (bell) pepper over a high heat for 1 minute. Stir in the aubergine (eggplant) pieces and stir-fry for a further minute, or until softened.

3 Stir in the sweetcorn and mangetout (snow peas) and stir-fry for about 1 minute. Add the mustard greens, mushrooms and beansprouts and stir-fry for 30 seconds.

4 Mix together the rice wine, yellow bean sauce, soy sauce, chilli sauce and sugar and add to the pan with the stock. Bring to the boil, stirring.

5 Slowly blend the cornflour (cornstarch) with the water to form a smooth paste. Stir quickly into the pan or wok and cook for a further minute. Serve immediately.

Potatoes in Creamed Coconut

A colourful way to serve potatoes which is quick and easy to make.
Serve it with spicy meat curries with a salad on the side.

Serves 4

INGREDIENTS

600 g/1 lb 5 oz potatoes
1 onion, thinly sliced
2 red bird-eye chillies, finely chopped
½ tsp salt

½ tsp ground black pepper
80 g/3 oz/½ cup creamed coconut
350 ml/12 fl oz/1½ cups vegetable or
chicken stock

fresh coriander (cilantro) or basil,
chopped, to garnish

1 Peel the potatoes thinly. Use a sharp knife to cut into 2 cm/¾ inch chunks.

2 Place the potatoes in a pan with the onion, chillies, salt, pepper and creamed coconut. Stir in the stock.

3 Bring to the boil, stirring, then lower the heat, cover and simmer gently, stirring occasionally, until the potatoes are tender.

4 Adjust the seasoning to taste, then sprinkle with chopped coriander (cilantro) or basil. Serve immediately while hot.

COOK'S TIP

If the potatoes are a thin-skinned, or a new variety, simply wash or scrub to remove any dirt and cook with the skins on. This adds extra dietary fibre and nutrients to the finished dish, and cuts down on the preparation time. Baby new potatoes can be cooked whole.

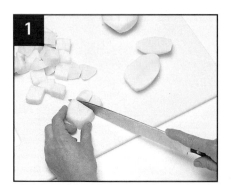

Stir-fried Broccoli in Oyster Sauce

Chinese oyster sauce has a sweet-salty flavour, ideal for adding a richly Oriental flavour to plain vegetables. Try this recipe with fresh asparagus when it's in season.

Serves 4

INGREDIENTS

400 g/14 oz broccoli
1 tbsp groundnut oil
2 shallots, finely chopped

1 garlic clove, finely chopped
1 tbsp rice wine or sherry
5 tbsp oyster sauce

¼ tsp ground black pepper
1 tsp chilli oil

1 Trim the broccoli and cut into small florets. Blanch in a pan of boiling water for about 30 seconds, then drain well.

2 Heat the oil in a large frying pan (skillet) or wok and stir-fry the shallots and garlic for 1–2 minutes until golden brown.

3 Stir in the broccoli and stir-fry for 2 minutes. Add the rice wine and oyster sauce and stir for a further 1 minute.

4 Stir in the pepper and drizzle with a little chilli oil just before serving.

COOK'S TIP

To make chilli oil, tuck fresh red or green chillies into a jar and top up with olive oil or a light vegetable oil. Cover with a lid and leave to infuse the flavour for at least 3 weeks before using.

Roasted Thai-spiced Peppers

A colourful side dish that also makes a good buffet party salad.
This is best made in advance to give time for the flavours to mingle.

Serves 4

INGREDIENTS

2 red (bell) peppers
2 yellow (bell) peppers
2 green (bell) peppers

2 red bird-eye chillies, deseeded and
 finely chopped
1 lemon grass stalk (stem), finely
 shredded

4 tbsp lime juice
2 tbsp palm sugar
1 tbsp Thai fish sauce

1 Roast the peppers under a hot grill (broiler), barbecue over hot coals or roast in a hot oven, turning them over occasionally, until the skins are charred. Cool slightly, then remove the skins. Cut each in half and remove the core and seeds.

2 Slice the peppers thickly and transfer to a large mixing bowl.

3 Place the chillies, lemon grass, lime juice, sugar and fish sauce in a screw-top jar and shake well until thoroughly mixed.

4 Pour the dressing evenly over the peppers. Allow to cool completely, cover with cling film (plastic wrap) and chill in the refrigerator for at least an hour before serving. Transfer to a serving dish to serve.

COOK'S TIP

The flavours will mingle best if the peppers are still slightly warm when you spoon the dressing over. Prepare the dressing while the peppers are cooking, so it's ready to pour over when they are cooked.

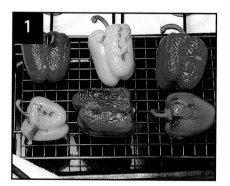

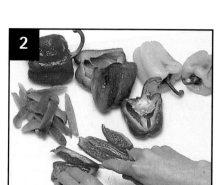

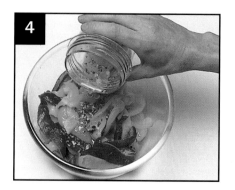

Pak Choi with Crab Meat

Pak choi, also called bok choi, Chinese greens or Chinese chard, has a delicate, fresh flavour and crisp texture, which is best retained by light, quick cooking. This makes it an ideal choice for stir-frying.

Serves 4

INGREDIENTS

2 heads green pak choi, about 250 g/
   9 oz total weight
2 tbsp vegetable oil
1 garlic clove, thinly sliced

2 tbsp oyster sauce
100 g/3½ oz/1 cup cherry tomatoes,
   halved

170 g/6 oz can white crab meat,
   drained
salt and pepper

1 Trim the pak choi and cut into 2.5 cm/1 inch thick slices.

2 Heat the oil in a large frying pan (skillet) or wok and stir-fry the garlic quickly over a high heat for 1 minute.

3 Add the pak choi and stir-fry for 2–3 minutes until the leaves wilt, but the stalks (stems) are still crisp.

4 Add the oyster sauce and tomatoes and stir-fry for a further minute.

5 Add the crab meat and season well with salt and pepper. Stir to heat thoroughly and break up the distribution of crab meat before serving.

VARIATION

For a vegetarian version of this dish, omit the crab meat and replace the oyster sauce with 2 tablespoons of light soy sauce.

VARIATION

If pak choi is not available, Chinese leaves (cabbage) make a good alternative for this dish.

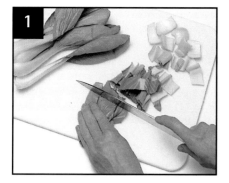

Spiced Cashew Nut Curry

*This unusual vegetarian dish is best served as a side dish
with other curries, either vegetable or meat-based, with rice to soak up
the wonderfully rich, spiced juices.*

Serves 4

INGREDIENTS

250 g/9 oz/1½ cups unsalted cashew
  nuts
1 tsp coriander seeds
1 tsp cumin seeds
2 cardamom pods, crushed
1 tbsp sunflower oil

1 onion, finely sliced
1 garlic clove, crushed
1 small green chilli, deseeded and
  chopped
1 cinnamon stick
½ tsp ground turmeric

4 tbsp coconut cream
300 ml/10 fl oz/1¼ cups hot
  vegetable stock
3 kaffir lime leaves, finely shredded
salt and pepper
boiled jasmine rice, to serve

1 Soak the cashew nuts in cold
water overnight. Drain
thoroughly. Crush the coriander,
cumin seeds and cardamom pods
in a pestle and mortar.

2 Heat the oil and stir-fry the
onion and garlic for 2–3
minutes to soften, but not brown.
Add the chilli, crushed spices,
cinnamon stick and turmeric, and
stir-fry for a further minute.

3 Add the coconut cream and
the hot stock to the pan. Bring
to the boil, then add the cashew
nuts and lime leaves.

4 Cover the pan, lower the heat
and simmer for about 20
minutes. Serve hot, accompanied
by jasmine rice.

COOK'S TIP

*All spices give the best
flavour when freshly
crushed, but if you prefer,
you can use ground spices
instead of crushing them yourself in
a pestle and mortar.*

Potato & Spinach Yellow Curry

Potatoes are not highly regarded in Thai cookery, as rice is the traditional staple. This dish is a tasty exception, and with its luxuriously creamy, golden coconut sauce, it makes a superb side dish for any meal.

Serves 4

INGREDIENTS

2 garlic cloves, finely chopped

3 cm/1¼ inch piece galangal, finely chopped

1 lemon grass stalk (stem), finely chopped

1 tsp coriander seeds

3 tbsp vegetable oil

2 tsp Thai red curry paste

½ tsp turmeric

200 ml/7 fl oz/scant 1 cup coconut milk

250 g/9 oz potatoes, peeled and cut into 2 cm/¾ inch cubes

100 ml/3½ fl oz/scant ½ cup vegetable stock

200 g/7 oz/3 cups young spinach leaves

1 small onion, thinly sliced into rings

1 Place the garlic, galangal, lemon grass and coriander seeds in a pestle and mortar and pound until a smooth paste forms.

2 Heat 2 tablespoons of the oil in a frying pan (skillet) or wok. Stir in the paste and stir-fry for 30 seconds. Stir in the curry paste and turmeric, then add the coconut milk and bring to the boil.

3 Add the potatoes and stock. Return to the boil, then lower the heat and simmer, uncovered, for 10–12 minutes until the potatoes are almost tender.

4 Stir in the spinach and simmer until the leaves are wilted.

5 Meanwhile, fry the onions in the remaining oil until crisp and golden brown. Place on top of the curry just before serving.

COOK'S TIP

Choose a firm, waxy potato for this dish, one that will keep its shape during cooking in preference to a floury variety which will break up easily once cooked.

Sweet Potato Cakes with Soy-tomato Sauce

Enticing little tasty mouthfuls of sweet potato, served hot and sizzling from the pan with a delicious fresh tomato sauce.

Serves 4

INGREDIENTS

2 sweet potatoes, 500 g/1 lb 2 oz
  total weight
2 garlic cloves, crushed
1 small green chilli, chopped
2 sprigs coriander (cilantro), chopped
1 tbsp dark soy sauce

plain (all-purpose) flour for shaping
vegetable oil for frying
sesame seeds for sprinkling

SOY-TOMATO SAUCE:
2 tsp vegetable oil
1 garlic clove, finely chopped

2 cm/¾ inch piece fresh ginger root,
  finely chopped
3 tomatoes, skinned and chopped
2 tbsp dark soy sauce
1 tbsp lime juice
2 tbsp fresh coriander (cilantro),
  chopped

1 Make the soy-tomato sauce. Heat the oil in a wok and stir-fry the garlic and ginger for about 1 minute. Add the tomatoes and stir-fry for a further 2 minutes. Remove from the heat and stir in the soy sauce, lime and coriander. Set aside and keep warm.

2 Peel the sweet potatoes and grate finely (you can do this quickly with a food processor). Place the garlic, chilli and coriander (cilantro) in a pestle and mortar and crush to a smooth paste. Stir in the soy sauce mix with the sweet potatoes.

3 Divide the mixture into 12 equal portions. Dip into flour and pat into a flat round patty shape.

4 Heat a shallow layer of oil in a wide frying pan (skillet). Fry the sweet potato patties over a high heat until golden, turning once.

5 Drain on paper towels and sprinkle with sesame seeds. Serve hot, with a spoonful of the soy-tomato sauce.

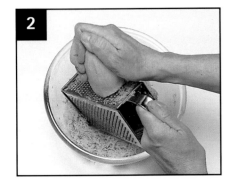

Thai-style Sweetcorn Fritters

These quick, little fritters can be served as a side dish or a first course, with a spoonful of spicy chilli relish and a squeeze of lime juice.

Serves 4

INGREDIENTS

55 g/2 oz/½ cup plain
   (all purpose) flour
1 large egg
2 tsp Thai green curry paste
5 tbsp coconut milk
400 g/14 oz/2¼ cups canned or
   frozen sweetcorn (corn) kernels

4 spring onions (scallions)
1 tbsp fresh coriander (cilantro),
   chopped
1 tbsp fresh basil, chopped
salt and pepper
vegetable oil for shallow frying

TO SERVE:
lime wedges
chilli relish

1 Place the flour, egg, curry paste, coconut milk and about half the sweetcorn kernels in a food processor and process until a smooth, thick batter forms.

2 Finely chop the spring onions (scallions) and stir into the batter with the remaining sweetcorn, chopped coriander (cilantro) and basil. Season well with salt and pepper.

3 Heat a small amount of oil in a wide, heavy-based frying pan (skillet). Drop in tablespoonfuls of the batter and cook for 2–3 minutes until golden brown.

4 Turn them over and cook for a further 2–3 minutes until golden. Fry in batches, making about 12–16 fritters, keeping the cooked fritters hot while you cook the remaining batter.

5 Serve the fritters hot, with lime wedges and a chilli relish.

COOK'S TIP

If you prefer to use fresh sweetcorn, strip the kernels from the cobs with a sharp knife, then cook in boiling water for about 4–5 minutes until just tender. Drain well before using as instructed.

Spicy Vegetable Fritters with Sweet Chilli Dip

These spicy fritters show a clear Indian influence, as they are very similar to pakoras, which are spicy Indian vegetable fritters. They can be served as a first course or as a side dish. The sweet chilli dip is a perfect partner.

Serves 4–6

INGREDIENTS

150 g/5½ oz/1 cup plain (all-purpose) flour
1 tsp ground coriander
1 tsp ground cumin
1 tsp turmeric
1 tsp salt
½ tsp ground black pepper
2 garlic cloves, finely chopped
3 cm/1¼ inch piece fresh ginger root, chopped

2 small green chillies, finely chopped
1 tbsp fresh coriander (cilantro), chopped
about 225 ml/8 fl oz/1 cup water
1 onion, chopped
1 potato, coarsely grated
80 g/3 oz/½ cup sweetcorn kernels
1 small aubergine (eggplant), diced
125 g/4½ oz/1 cup Chinese broccoli, cut into short lengths

coconut oil for deep frying

SWEET CHILLI DIP:
2 red bird-eye chillies, finely chopped
4 tbsp caster (superfine) sugar
4 tbsp rice vinegar
1 tbsp light soy sauce

1 Make the dip by mixing together all the ingredients thoroughly until the sugar is dissolved. Cover and set aside until needed.

2 For the fritters, place the flour in a bowl and stir in the coriander, cumin, turmeric, salt and pepper. Add the garlic, ginger, chillies and coriander (cilantro) with just enough cold water to make a thick batter.

3 Add the onion, potato, sweetcorn, aubergine (eggplant) and broccoli to the batter and stir well to distribute the ingredients evenly.

4 Heat the oil in a wok to 190°C/375°F, or until a cube of bread browns in 30 seconds. Drop tablespoons of the batter into the hot oil and fry in batches until golden and crisp, turning once.

5 Fry in batches, if necessary. Keep the first batches of fried fritters hot in a warm oven whilst cooking the others. Drain well on paper towels and serve at once while still hot, accompanied by the sweet chilli dip.

Aubergine- & Mushroom-stuffed Omelette

In Thailand, egg dishes such as this one are eaten as main dishes or snacks, depending on the time of day.

Serves 1–2

INGREDIENTS

3 tbsp vegetable oil
1 garlic clove, finely chopped
1 small onion, finely chopped
1 small aubergine (eggplant), diced
½ small green (bell) pepper, deseeded
    and chopped

1 large dried Chinese black
    mushroom, soaked, drained and
    sliced
1 tomato, diced
1 tbsp light soy sauce
½ tsp sugar

¼ tsp ground black pepper
2 large eggs
salad leaves, tomato wedges and
    cucumber slices, to garnish

1 Heat half the oil and fry the garlic over a high heat for 30 seconds. Add the onion and the aubergine (eggplant) and continue to stir-fry until golden.

2 Add the green (bell) pepper and stir-fry for a further minute to soften. Stir in the mushroom, tomato, soy sauce, sugar and pepper. Remove from the pan and keep hot.

3 Beat the eggs together lightly. Heat the remaining oil, swirling to coat a wide area. Pour in the egg and swirl to set around the pan.

4 When the egg is set, spoon the filling into the centre. Fold in the sides of the omelette to make a square parcel.

5 Slide the omelette carefully on to a warmed dish and garnish with salad leaves, tomato wedges and cucumber slices. Serve hot.

COOK'S TIP

If you heat the pan thoroughly before adding the oil, and heat the oil before adding the ingredients, you should not have a problem with ingredients sticking to the pan.

Crispy Tofu with Chilli-soy Sauce

Tempting golden cubes of fried tofu, with colourful fresh carrot and peppers, combine with a warm ginger sauce to make an unusual side dish or light lunch dish.

Serves 4

INGREDIENTS

300 g/10½ oz firm tofu
2 tbsp vegetable oil
1 garlic clove, sliced
1 carrot, cut into matchsticks
½ green (bell) pepper, deseeded and
    cut into matchsticks

1 red bird-eye chilli, deseeded and
    finely chopped
2 tbsp soy sauce
1 tbsp lime juice
1 tbsp Thai fish sauce
1 tbsp soft light brown sugar

pickled garlic slices, to serve
    (optional)

1 Drain the tofu and pat dry with paper towels. Cut into 2 cm/¾ inch cubes.

2 Heat the oil in a wok and stir-fry the garlic for 1 minute. Remove the garlic and add the tofu, then fry quickly until well-browned, turning gently to brown on all sides.

3 Lift out the tofu, drain well and keep hot. Stir the carrot and pepper into the pan and stir-fry for 1 minute.

4 Spoon the carrot and peppers on to a dish and pile the tofu on top.

5 Mix together the chilli, soy sauce, lime juice, fish sauce and sugar, stirring until the sugar is dissolved.

6 Spoon the same over the tofu and serve topped with slices of pickled garlic, if you like. Serve hot.

COOK'S TIP

Make sure to buy firm fresh tofu for this dish – the softer 'silken' type is more like junket in texture and not firm enough to hold its shape well during frying. It is better for adding to soups.

Cucumber Salad

*This refreshing spicy salad makes an excellent accompaniment for spicy
grilled (broiled) fish and meat dishes.*

Serves 4

INGREDIENTS

1 cucumber
salt and pepper
1 small red onion

1 garlic clove, crushed
½ tsp chilli paste
2 tsp Thai fish sauce

1 tbsp lime juice
1 tsp sesame oil

1 Trim the cucumber and
coarsely grate the flesh. Place
in a sieve (strainer) over a bowl,
sprinkle with 1 teaspoon salt and
leave to drain for 20 minutes.
Discard the liquid.

2 Peel the onion and chop
finely, then toss into the
cucumber. Spoon into 4 individual
bowls or one large one.

3 Mix together the garlic, chilli
paste, fish sauce, lime juice
and sesame oil, then spoon over
the salad. Cover the salad and chill
before serving.

VARIATION

*For a change, peel
the cucumber and cut
it into small dice, then
salt and drain as above.
Drain and toss with the onions
and dressing as before.*

COOK'S TIP

*Once the salad is made, it can be
chilled with the dressing for 1–2 hours,
but is best eaten on the day of making.*

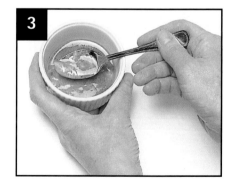

Thai Green Salad

An unusual side salad that is a good accompaniment to any simple Thai main dish, especially grilled (broiled) meats and fish. Add the dressing just before serving or the leaves will lose their crispness.

Serves 4–6

INGREDIENTS

1 small head Cos (romaine) lettuce
1 bunch spring onions (scallions)
½ cucumber
4 tbsp fresh coconut, toasted, coarsely shredded

DRESSING:
4 tbsp lime juice
2 tbsp Thai fish sauce
1 small red bird-eye chilli, finely chopped

1 tsp sugar
1 garlic clove, crushed
2 tbsp fresh coriander (cilantro), chopped
1 tbsp fresh mint, chopped

1 Tear or roughly shred the lettuce leaves and place in a large salad bowl.

2 Trim and thinly slice the spring onions (scallions) diagonally, then add them to the salad bowl.

3 Use a vegetable peeler to shave thin slices along the length of the cucumber and add to the salad bowl.

4 Place all the ingredients for the dressing in a screw-top jar, close the lid tightly and shake well to mix thoroughly.

5 Pour the dressing over the salad and toss well to coat the leaves evenly.

6 Scatter the coconut over the salad and toss in lightly just before serving.

COOK'S TIP

This salad is good for picnics – to pack it easily, pack the leaves into a large polythene (plastic) container or unbreakable salad bowl, and nestle the jar of dressing in the centre. Cover with cling film (plastic wrap). Packed this way, the salad stays crisp and if the dressing leaks during transit, there's no mess.

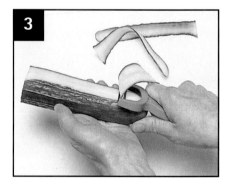

Grilled Aubergine & Sesame Salad

*Aubergines (eggplants) are a popular vegetable in Thailand,
as they grow easily throughout the Far East. This dish works well as a first course,
but can also be served as an accompaniment to fish or meat dishes.*

Serves 4

INGREDIENTS

8 baby aubergines (eggplants)
salt
2 tsp chilli oil
1 tbsp soy sauce
1 tbsp Thai fish sauce

1 garlic clove, thinly sliced
1 red bird-eye chilli, deseeded and
   sliced
1 tbsp sunflower oil
1 tsp sesame oil

1 tbsp lime juice
1 tsp soft light brown sugar
1 tbsp fresh mint, chopped
1 tbsp sesame seeds, toasted
mint leaves, to garnish

1 Cut the aubergines (eggplants) lengthways into thin slices to within 2.5 cm/1 inch of the stem end. Place in a colander, sprinkling with salt between the slices and leave to drain for about 30 minutes. Rinse in cold water and pat dry with paper towels.

2 Mix the chilli oil, soy sauce and fish sauce together, and then brush over the aubergines (eggplants). Cook under a hot grill (broiler), or barbecue over hot coals, for 6–8 minutes, turning them over occasionally and brushing with more chilli oil glaze, until golden brown and softened. Arrange them on a serving platter.

3 Fry the garlic and chilli in the sunflower oil for 1–2 minutes until just beginning to brown. Remove the pan from the heat and add the sesame oil, lime juice, brown sugar and any spare chilli oil glaze.

4 Add the chopped mint and spoon the warm dressing over the aubergines (eggplants).

5 Leave to marinate for about 20 minutes, then sprinkle with toasted sesame seeds. Serve garnished with mint.

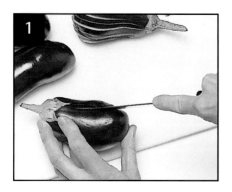

Oriental Lettuce Cups

*A crisp salad with a rich and warmly spiced coconut and peanut dressing,
served in pretty lettuce cups.*

Serves 4

INGREDIENTS

8 leaves Cos (romaine) lettuce, or
    similar firm lettuce leaves
2 carrots
2 celery sticks
100 g/3½ oz baby sweetcorn
2 spring onions (scallions)
100 g/3½ oz/1 cup beansprouts

2 tbsp roasted peanuts, chopped

DRESSING:
2 tbsp smooth peanut butter
3 tbsp lime juice
3 tbsp coconut milk
2 tsp Thai fish sauce

1 tsp caster (super fine) sugar
1 tsp fresh ginger root, grated
¼ tsp Thai red curry paste

1 Wash and trim the lettuce
leaves, leaving them whole.
Arrange on a serving plate or on
individual plates.

2 Trim the carrots and
celery and cut into fine
matchsticks. Trim the sweetcorn
(corn) and onions and slice
both diagonally.

3 Toss together all the
prepared vegetables with
the beansprouts. Divide the
salad mixture evenly between
the individual lettuce cups.

4 To make the dressing, place
all the ingredients in a
screw-top jar and shake well
until thoroughly mixed.

5 Spoon the dressing evenly
over the salad cups and
sprinkle with chopped peanuts.
Serve immediately.

COOK'S TIP

*Choose leaves with a deep cup
shape to hold the salad neatly. If
you prefer, Chinese leaves may be
used in place of the Cos (romaine)
lettuce. To remove the leaves from
the whole head without tearing
them, cut a thick slice from the base
end so the leaves are not attached by
their stems, then gently ease away
the leafy parts.*

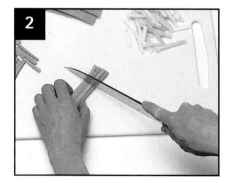

Thai-style Carrot & Mango Salad

A wonderfully refreshing, simple salad to serve as a side dish with hot and spicy meat or fish dishes. It can be prepared an hour or two in advance of serving, and chilled in the refrigerator until needed.

Serves 4

INGREDIENTS

4 carrots
1 small, ripe mango
200 g/7 oz firm tofu
1 tbsp fresh chives, chopped

DRESSING:
2 tbsp orange juice
1 tbsp lime juice
1 tsp clear honey

½ tsp orange-flower water
1 tsp sesame oil
1 tsp sesame seeds, toasted

1 Peel and coarsely grate the carrots. Peel, stone (seed) and thinly slice the mango.

2 Cut the tofu into 1 cm/½ inch dice-shaped pieces and toss together with the carrots and mango in a wide salad bowl.

3 For the dressing, place all the ingredients in a screw-top jar and shake well to mix evenly.

4 Pour the dressing over the salad and toss well to coat the salad evenly.

5 Just before serving, toss the salad lightly and sprinkle with chives. Serve immediately.

COOK'S TIP

A food processor will grate the carrots in seconds, and is especially useful for time-saving if you're catering for a crowd.

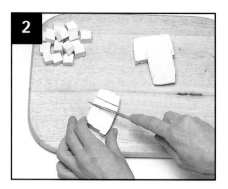

Bamboo Shoot Salad

In Thailand, fresh bamboo would always be used for this salad, but canned bamboo shoots make a very good alternative. This dish is usually served to accompany roast pork.

Serves 4

INGREDIENTS

2 shallots
2 garlic cloves
2 tbsp Thai fish sauce
3 tbsp lime juice
½ tsp dried chilli flakes

1 tsp granulated sugar
1 tbsp round-grain rice
2 tsp sesame seeds
350 g/12 oz can bamboo shoots, drained

2 spring onions (scallions), chopped
Chinese leaves or lettuce, shredded, to serve
mint leaves, to garnish

1 Place the whole shallots and garlic under a medium-hot grill and grill (broil) until charred on the outside and tender inside. Remove the skins and place the flesh in a pestle and mortar. Crush to a smooth paste.

2 Mix the paste with the fish sauce, lime juice, chilli flakes and sugar.

3 Place the rice and sesame seeds in a heavy-based frying pan (skillet) over the heat and cook to a rich golden brown, shaking the pan to brown evenly. Remove from the heat and crush lightly in a pestle and mortar.

4 Use a sharp knife to shred the bamboo shoots into fine matchsticks. Stir in the shallot and garlic dressing, tossing well to coat the mixture evenly. Stir in the toasted rice and sesame seeds, then the spring onions (scallions).

5 Pile the salad on to a serving dish and surround with shredded Chinese leaves. Garnish with mint leaves and serve.

Hot & Sour Beef Salad

Thais are primarily fish-eaters, so beef usually only appears on the menu for feast days. But, as in this dish, a little can go a long way and Thais expertly extend it with exotic mixes of herbs, spices and colourful vegetables.

Serves 4

INGREDIENTS

1 tsp black peppercorns
1 tsp coriander seeds
1 dried red bird-eye chilli
¼ tsp five-spice powder
250 g/9 oz beef fillet (tenderloin)
1 tbsp dark soy sauce
6 spring onions (scallions)
1 carrot

¼ cucumber
8 radishes
1 red onion
¼ head Chinese leaves
2 tbsp groundnut oil
1 garlic clove, crushed
1 tsp lemon grass, finely chopped
1 tbsp fresh mint, chopped

1 tbsp fresh coriander, chopped

DRESSING:
3 tbsp lime juice
1 tbsp light soy sauce
2 tsp soft light brown sugar
1 tsp sesame oil

1 Crush the peppercorns, coriander seeds and chilli in a pestle and mortar, then mix with the five-spice powder and sprinkle on a plate. Brush the beef all over with soy sauce, then roll it in the spices to coat evenly.

2 Cut the spring onions (scallions) into 6 cm/2½ inch lengths and then shred them finely lengthways. Place in iced water and leave until curled. Drain well.

3 Trim the carrot and cut into very thin diagonal slices. Halve the cucumber and scoop out the seeds, then slice thinly. Trim the radishes and cut into flower shapes.

4 Slice the onion thinly, cutting each slice from top to root.

Roughly shred the Chinese leaves. Toss all the vegetables together in a large salad bowl.

5 Heat the oil in a heavy-based frying pan (skillet) and fry the garlic and lemon grass until just turning golden brown. Add the steak and press down with a spatula to ensure it browns evenly. Cook for 3–4 minutes, turning it over once, depending on the thickness. Remove the pan from the heat.

6 Slice the steak thinly and toss into the salad with the mint and coriander (cilantro). Mix together the dressing ingredients and stir into the pan, then spoon over the salad. Serve immediately.

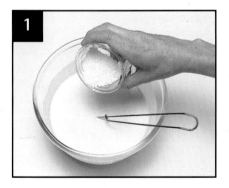

Mung Bean Custards

Mung beans give this sweet custard an unusual texture, and it's a real treat served with a generous dollop of crème fraîche.

Serves 6

INGREDIENTS

125 g/4½ oz/⅔ cup dried mung beans
2 eggs, beaten
175 ml/6 fl oz/¾ cup coconut milk

100 g/3½ oz/½ cup caster (superfine) sugar
1 tbsp ground rice
1 tsp ground cinnamon

TO DECORATE:
ground cinnamon
crème fraîche or whipped cream
lime rind, finely grated
starfruit, sliced
pomegranate seeds

1 Place the beans in a saucepan with enough water to cover. Bring to the boil, then lower the heat to simmer for 30–40 minutes until the beans are very tender. Drain well.

2 Mash the beans, then press through a sieve to make a smooth purée. Place the bean purée, eggs, coconut milk, sugar, rice flour and cinnamon in a large bowl and beat well until mixed.

3 Grease and base-line four 150 ml/5 fl oz/⅔ cup pudding-shaped moulds or ramekin dishes and pour in the mixture. Place on a baking sheet in a preheated oven at 180°C/350°F/Gas Mark 4 and bake for 20–25 minutes or until just set.

4 Cool the custards in the moulds, then run a knife around the edge to loosen and turn out on to a serving plate. Sprinkle with cinnamon. Top with a spoonful of crème fraîche or whipped cream and serve with exotic fruit.

COOK'S TIP

To save time use canned mung beans. Omit Step 1, drain the beans thoroughly and continue with step 2.

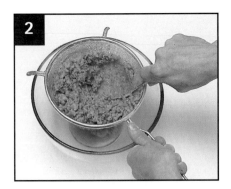

Banana Fritters in Coconut Batter

*This irresistible, classic dessert is best served with a squeeze of lime juice,
and topped with a generous spoonful rich vanilla ice cream.*

Serves 4

INGREDIENTS

70 g/2½ oz/9 tbsp plain (all-purpose)
   flour
2 tbsp rice flour
1 tbsp caster (superfine) sugar

1 egg, separated
150 ml/5 fl oz/⅔ cup coconut milk
4 large bananas
sunflower oil for deep frying

TO DECORATE:
1 tsp icing (confectioners') sugar
1 tsp ground cinnamon
lime wedges

1 Sift the plain (all-purpose) flour, rice flour and sugar into a bowl and make a well in the centre. Add the egg yolk and coconut milk.

2 Beat the mixture until a smooth, thick batter forms. Whisk the egg white in a clean, dry bowl until stiff enough to hold soft peaks. Fold it into the batter lightly and evenly.

3 Heat a 6 cm/2½ inch depth of oil in a large pan to 180°C/ 350°F, or until a cube of bread browns in 30 seconds. Cut the bananas in half crossways, then dip them quickly into the batter to coat them.

4 Drop the bananas carefully into the hot oil and fry in batches for 2–3 minutes until golden brown, turning once.

5 Drain on paper towels. Sprinkle with icing (confectioners') sugar and cinnamon and serve immediately, with lime wedges for squeezing juice as desired.

COOK'S TIP

If you can buy the baby finger bananas that are popular in this dish in the East, leave them whole for coating and frying.

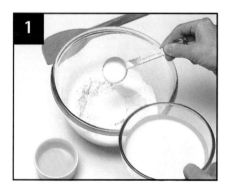

Bananas in Coconut Milk

An unusual dessert which is equally good served hot or cold.
The Thais like to combine fruits and vegetables, so it's not unusual to find
mung beans or sweetcorn mixed with bananas or other fruits.

Serves 4

INGREDIENTS

4 large bananas
350 ml/12 fl oz/1½ cups coconut milk
2 tbsp caster (superfine) sugar

pinch of salt
½ tsp orange-flower water
1 tbsp fresh mint, shredded

2 tbsp mung beans, cooked
mint sprigs, to decorate

1 Peel the bananas and cut them into short chunks. Place in a large pan with the coconut milk, caster (superfine) sugar and salt.

2 Heat gently until boiling and simmer for 1 minute. Remove from the heat.

3 Sprinkle the orange-flower water over, stir in the mint and spoon into a serving dish.

4 Place the mung beans in a heavy-based frying pan (skillet) and place over a high heat until turning crisp and golden, shaking the pan occasionally. Remove and crush lightly in a pestle and mortar.

5 Sprinkle the toasted beans over the bananas and serve warm or cold, decorated with fresh mint sprigs.

COOK'S TIP

If you prefer, the mung beans could be replaced with flaked, toasted almonds or hazelnuts.

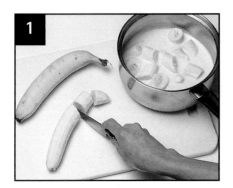

Caramel Apple Wedges with Sesame Seeds

A Thai version of a Chinese dessert, these sweet caramel-coated pieces of fruit take practice to perfect, but the trick is to get the timing right. Bananas can also be cooked in this way.

Serves 4

INGREDIENTS

115 g/4 oz/1 cup rice flour
1 egg
125 ml/4 fl oz/½ cup cold water
4 crisp dessert apples

2½ tbsp sesame seeds
250 g/9 oz/1¼ cups caster (superfine) sugar

2 tbsp vegetable oil
extra vegetable oil for deep frying

1 Place the flour, egg and water in a bowl and whisk well until a smooth, thick batter forms.

2 Core the apples and cut each into 8 wedges. Drop into the batter and stir in the sesame seeds.

3 Put the sugar and 2 tablespoons of oil in a heavy-based pan and heat, stirring, until the sugar dissolves. Continue until the syrup begins to turn golden. Remove from the heat but keep warm.

4 Heat the oil for frying in a wok or deep pan to 180°C/ 350°F, or until a cube of bread turns golden brown in 30 seconds. Lift the apple pieces one by one from the batter, using tongs and lower into the hot oil.

5 Fry for 2–3 minutes until golden brown and crisp.

6 Remove with a perforated spoon and dip very quickly into the sugar mixture. Dip the apple wedges briefly into iced water and drain on non-stick paper. Serve immediately.

COOK'S TIP

Take care not to overheat the sugar syrup or it will become difficult to handle and burn. If it begins to set before you have finished dipping the apple pieces, warm it slightly over the heat until it becomes liquid again.

Thai Rice Pudding

This Thai-style version of rice pudding is mildly spiced and creamy, with a rich custard topping.
It's excellent served warm, and even better the next day served cold –
in Thailand it's even served for breakfast.

Serves 4

INGREDIENTS

100 g/3½ oz/½ cup short-grain rice
2 tbsp palm sugar
1 cardamom pod, split
300 ml/10 fl oz/1¼ cups coconut milk

150 ml/5 fl oz/⅔ cup water
3 eggs
200 ml/7 fl oz/scant 1 cup coconut cream

1½ tbsp caster (superfine) sugar
fresh fruit, to serve
sweetened coconut flakes, to decorate

1 Place the rice and palm sugar in a pan. Crush the seeds from the cardamom pod in a pestle and mortar and add to the pan. Stir in the coconut milk and water.

2 Bring to the boil, stirring to dissolve the sugar. Lower the heat and simmer, uncovered, stirring occasionally for about 20 minutes until the rice is tender and most of the liquid is absorbed.

3 Spoon the rice into 4 individual ovenproof dishes and spread evenly. Place the dishes in a wide roasting tin (pan) with water to come about halfway up the sides.

4 Beat together the eggs, coconut cream and caster (superfine) sugar and spoon over the rice. Cover with foil and bake in a preheated oven to 180°C/350°F/Gas Mark 4 for 45–50 minutes until the custard sets.

5 Serve the rice puddings warm or cold, with fresh fruit and decorated with coconut flakes.

COOK'S TIP

Cardamom is quite a powerful spice, so if you find it too strong it can be left out altogether, or replaced with a little ground cinnamon.

Sticky Rice Balls

Glutinous rice is the base for many Thai desserts, and these little rice balls are typical.
They're often prettily coloured with food colourings and soaked in flower-scented syrups,
and children love them.

Serves 4

INGREDIENTS

300 g/10½ oz/1½ cups glutinous rice
500 g/1 lb 2oz/2½ cups granulated
  sugar
300 ml/10 fl oz/1¼ cups water

pink and green food colourings
few drops of rose water or jasmine
  essence

rose petals or jasmine flowers, to
  decorate

1 Place the rice in a bowl and add enough cold water to cover. Leave to soak for 3 hours, or overnight.

2 Drain the rice and rinse thoroughly in cold water.

3 Line the top part of a steamer with muslin (cheesecloth) and tip the rice into it. Place over boiling water, cover and steam the rice for 30 minutes. Remove and cool.

4 Heat the sugar and water gently until the sugar dissolves. Bring to the boil and boil for 4–5 minutes to reduce to a thin syrup. Remove the pan from the heat.

5 Divide the rice in half and colour one half pale pink, the other half pale green. Shape into small balls.

6 Using 2 forks, dip the rice balls into the syrup. Drain off the excess syrup and pile on to a dish. Scatter with rose petals or jasmine flowers.

COOK'S TIP

If you prefer, the rice can be shaped in small sweet moulds or piled into small castle or turret shapes, like dariole moulds.

Balinese Banana Pancakes

These little stacks of rich banana pancakes, drizzled with fragrant lime juice, are quite irresistible any time of day!

Serves 6

INGREDIENTS

175 g/6 oz/1¼ cups plain (all-purpose) flour
pinch of salt
4 eggs, beaten

2 large, ripe bananas, peeled and mashed
300 ml/10 fl oz/1¼ cups coconut milk
vegetable oil, to fry

sliced banana, to decorate
6 tbsp lime juice
icing (confectioners') sugar
coconut cream, to serve

1 Place the flour, salt, eggs, bananas and coconut milk in a blender or food processor and process until a smooth batter forms. Alternatively, if you don't have a food processor, sift the flour and salt into a bowl and make a well in the centre, then add the remaining ingredients and beat well until smooth.

2 Chill the batter for an hour. Remove from the refrigerator and beat briefly again. Heat a small amount of oil in a small frying pan (skillet) until very hot.

3 Drop tablespoonfuls of batter into the pan. Cook until the pancakes are golden underneath.

4 Turn over and cook the other side until golden brown. Cook in batches until all the batter is used up, making about 36 pancakes. Remove and drain on paper towels.

5 Serve the pancakes in a stack, decorated with sliced bananas, sprinkled with lime juice and icing sugar and topped with a dollop of coconut cream.

COOK'S TIP

These little pancakes are best eaten hot and freshly cooked, so keep them hot in a low oven while the others are cooking.

Coconut Pancakes

These pretty, lacy-thin pancakes (crêpes) are sold by Thai street vendors, often coloured a delicate pale pink, or tinted green with the juice from pandanus leaves. Add a tiny drop of food colour if you like, but they look pretty good just as they are, especially served with fresh fruits.

Serves 4

INGREDIENTS

115 g/4 oz/1 cup rice flour
40 g/1½ oz/3 tbsp caster (superfine)
    sugar
pinch of salt

2 eggs
600 ml/1 pint/2½ cups coconut milk
4 tbsp desiccated (shredded) coconut
vegetable oil, to fry

fresh mango or banana, to serve
2 tbsp palm sugar, to decorate

1 Place the rice flour, sugar and salt in a bowl and add the eggs and coconut milk, whisking until a smooth batter forms. Alternatively, place all the ingredients in a blender and process to a smooth batter. Beat in half the coconut.

2 Heat a small amount of oil in a wide, heavy-based frying pan (skillet). Pour in a little batter, swirling the pan to cover the surface thinly and evenly. Cook until pale golden underneath.

3 Turn or toss the pancake and cook quickly to brown lightly on the other side.

4 Turn out the pancakes and keep hot while using the remaining batter to make a total of 8 pancakes.

5 Serve the pancakes folded or loosely rolled, with slices of mango or banana, and sprinkled with palm sugar and the remaining coconut, toasted.

COOK'S TIP

Rice flour gives the pancakes a light, smooth texture, but if it's not available, use ordinary plain (all-purpose) flour instead.

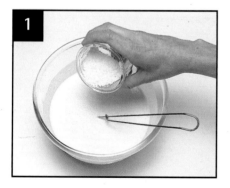

Steamed Coconut Cake with Lime & Ginger Syrup

This steamed coconut cake is very typical of Thai desserts and sweets, and has a distinctly Chinese influence. Eat it in small squares as it's quite rich and sweet.

Serves 8

INGREDIENTS

2 large (extra large) eggs, separated
pinch of salt
100 g/3½ oz/½ cup caster (superfine) sugar
75 g/2¾ oz/5 tbsp butter, melted and cooled
5 tbsp coconut milk

150 g/5½ oz/1¼ cups self-raising (self-rising) flour
½ tsp baking powder
3 tbsp desiccated (shredded) coconut
4 tbsp stem (candied) ginger syrup
3 tbsp lime juice

TO DECORATE:
3 pieces stem (candied) ginger
curls of fresh coconut, grated
lime rind, finely grated

1 Cut a 28 cm/11 inch round of non-stick paper and press into an 18 cm/7 inch steamer basket to line it.

2 Whisk the egg whites with the salt until stiff. Gradually whisk in the sugar, 1 tablespoon at a time, whisking hard after each addition until the mixture stands in stiff peaks.

3 Whisk in the yolks, then quickly stir in the butter and coconut milk. Sift the flour and baking powder over the mixture, then fold in lightly and evenly with a large metal spoon. Fold in the coconut.

4 Spoon the mixture into the lined steamer basket and tuck the spare paper over the top. Place the basket over boiling water, cover and steam for 30 minutes.

5 Turn out the cake on to a plate, remove the paper and cool slightly. Mix together the ginger and lime juice and spoon over the cake. Cut into squares and decorate with diced preserved stem (candied) ginger, curls of fresh coconut and lime rind.

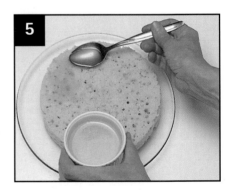

Strings of Gold

These golden egg threads take a little practice, but they're a very traditional Thai dessert, so well worth a try. The little coils of threads are meant to represent the hands placed together in a traditional Thai greeting. The Thais use a special tool to drizzle the egg in fine streams, but you can use a piping bag.

Serves 4

INGREDIENTS

7 egg yolks
1 tbsp egg white
500 g/1 lb 2 oz/2½ cups granulated
   sugar

200 ml/7 fl oz/scant 1 cup water
handful of scented jasmine flowers

TO SERVE:
pomegranate seeds
kiwi fruit, sliced
apple, sliced

1 Press the egg yolks and egg white through a fine sieve, then whisk lightly.

2 Place the sugar and water in a large pan and heat gently until the sugar dissolves. Add the jasmine flowers, bring to the boil and boil rapidly until a thin syrup forms. Remove the flowers with a perforated spoon.

3 Bring the syrup to the simmering point. Using a piping bag with a fine nozzle (tip), or a paper icing cone, quickly drizzle the egg mixture into the syrup in a thin stream to form loose nests or pyramid shapes.

4 As soon as the threads set, remove the nests carefully and drain well on paper towels. Arrange on a warmed serving dish, with the pomegranate seeds, kiwi fruit and apple. Serve at once.

COOK'S TIP

If you can't get hold of fresh, scented jasmine flowers, add a few drops of rosewater or orange-flower water to the syrup instead.

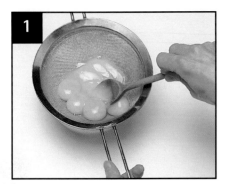

Melon & Ginger Crush

A really refreshing summer drink, this melon crush is quick and simple to make.
If you can't buy kaffir limes, ordinary lime are fine.

Serves 4

INGREDIENTS

1 melon, about 800 g/1 lb 12 oz
6 tbsp ginger wine

3 tbsp kaffir lime juice
ice, crushed

1 lime

1 Peel, deseed and roughly chop the melon. Place it in a blender or food processor with the ginger wine and lime juice.

2 Blend together on high speed until the melon mixture is completely smooth.

3 Put plenty of crushed ice into 4 tall tumblers. Pour the melon and ginger crush over the ice.

4 Cut the lime into slim slices, cut a slit in each one and slip it on to the side of each glass. Add a slice of lime to each glass as well. Serve immediately.

VARIATION

If you prefer a non-alcoholic version of this drink, simply omit the ginger wine, then top up with ginger ale in the glass. For a change of flavour, use a watermelon when they are in season. Ginger wine is available from specialist wine merchants or liquor stores.

Mango & Coconut Smoothie

A velvety-smooth, delicately scented drink without alcohol.
This can be served at any time of day – even for breakfast.

Serves 4

INGREDIENTS

2 large, ripe mangoes
1 tbsp icing (confectioners') sugar

500 ml/18 fl oz/2¼ cups coconut milk
5 ice cubes

toasted coconut, flaked, to serve

1 Cut the mangoes in half and remove the stone (seed). Cut away the peel and coarsley chop the flesh.

2 Place the chopped flesh in a blender goblet or food processor with the icing (confectioners') sugar and blend until completely smooth.

3 Add the coconut milk and ice to the blender or food processor and blend again until frothy.

4 Pour into 4 tall glasses and sprinkle with flaked, toasted coconut to serve.

COOK'S TIP

To add a special kick to the drink (though not perhaps for breakfast!), add a generous dash of white rum to the blender with the coconut milk.

VARIATION

If you don't have shredded, toasted coconut, sprinkle with ground ginger, cinamon or nutmeg just before serving.

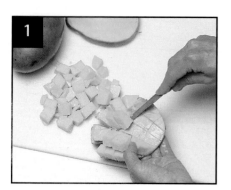

Lime & Lemon Grass Cooler

This cooling, non-alcoholic cocktail looks delightful served in tall glasses with frosted rims.
If you're after something stronger, add a shot of gin or vodka to each glass.

Serves 4

INGREDIENTS

egg white and caster (superfine)
  sugar, to frost
2 limes

1 small lemon grass stalk (stem)
3 tbsp caster (superfine) sugar
4 ice cubes

120 ml/4 fl oz/½ cup water
4 lime slices
soda water

1 To frost the rim of the glasses, pour a little egg white into a saucer. Dip the rim of each glass briefly into egg white and then into caster (superfine) sugar.

2 Cut each lime into 8 pieces and coarsely chop the lemon grass. Place the lime pieces and lemon grass in a blender or food processor with the sugar and ice cubes.

3 Add the water and process for a few seconds, but not until completely smooth.

4 Strain the mixture into the frosted glasses. Add a lime slice to each glass and top up to taste with soda water. Serve at once.

COOK'S TIP

It's important not to blend the limes for too long – a few seconds is enough to chop them finely and extract the juice. If you process too far, the drink will have a bitter flavour.

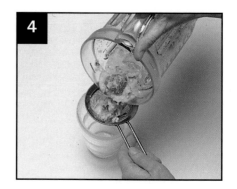

Thai Cocktail Sling

A Thai-style version of a much more classic cocktail, this is a long drink with a hefty kick of whisky.

Serves 1

INGREDIENTS

2 tbsp whisky
1 tbsp cherry brandy
1 tbsp orange-flavoured liqueur

1 tbsp lime juice
1 tsp palm sugar
dash of Angostura bitters

2 ice cubes
120 ml/4 fl oz/½ cup pineapple juice
small wedge pineapple

1 Place the whisky, cherry brandy, liqueur, lime juice, palm sugar and Angostura bitters in a cocktail shaker. Shake well to mix thoroughly.

2 Place the ice cubes in a large glass. Pour the cocktail mixture over the ice, then top up with the pineapple juice.

3 Cut a slit in the pineapple wedge and place on the edge of the glass. Serve immediately.

COOK'S TIP

If the pineapple juice is quite sweet, as Thai pineapple juice is, you may not need to add sugar. So if you're unsure, taste first.

COOK'S TIP

Scotch whisky is very highly regarded in Thailand, although a powerful whisky is distilled locally – if you have the stomach for it!

Tropical Fruit Punch

This exotic-looking cocktail is simplicity itself, and can be varied with different fruit juices.
Top with lavish amounts of fruit for a really festive effect.

Serves 6

INGREDIENTS

1 small ripe mango
4 tbsp lime juice
1 tsp fresh ginger root, finely grated
1 tbsp soft light brown sugar
300 ml/10 fl oz/1¼ cups orange juice

300 ml/10 fl oz/1¼ cups pineapple
juice
100 ml/3½ fl oz/scant ½ cup rum
ice, crushed

TO DECORATE:
starfruit slices
lime slices
pineapple slices

1 Peel and stone (seed) the mango and chop the flesh. Place in a blender or food processor with the lime juice, ginger and sugar and process until smooth.

2 Add the orange and pineapple juice, and then the rum and process again for a few seconds until blended.

3 Divide the crushed ice between 6 glasses and pour the punch over the ice.

4 Add orange and lime slices, then decorate the rim of each glass with pineapple and starfruit.

COOK'S TIP

To extend the drink a little further, and bring out the ginger flavour more, top up each glass with a generous dash of ginger ale.

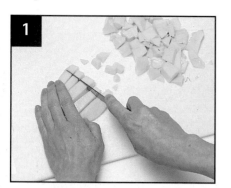

Index